Maple Sugaring

Maple Sugaring

KEEPING IT REAL
IN NEW ENGLAND

• • • • • • •

David K. Leff

Wesleyan University Press • Middletown, Connecticut

Wesleyan University Press
Middletown CT 06459
www.wesleyan.edu/wespress
© 2015 David K. Leff
All rights reserved
Manufactured in the United States of America
Designed by April Leidig
Typeset in Monotype Bell by Copperline Book Services

Wesleyan University Press is a member of the Green Press Initiative.
The paper used in this book meets their minimum
requirement for recycled paper.

Library of Congress Cataloging-in-Publication Data
Leff, David K., author.
Maple sugaring: keeping it real in New England / David K. Leff.
pages cm.—(Garnet books)
ISBN 978-0-8195-7569-2 (cloth: alk. paper)
ISBN 978-0-8195-7570-8 (ebook)
1. Maple sugar industry—New England. 2. Maple sugar—
New England. I. Title. II. Series: Garnet books.
HD9119.M32U54 2015
338.1′74972280974—dc23 2014048354

5 4 3 2 1

All recipes included in this volume were published in
The Maple Cookbook: Connecticut Style, compiled by the Maple
Syrup Producers Association of Connecticut and edited by
Jane Worthington (July 2012). Used with permission.

Contents

· · · · · · · · · · · · · · ·

Preface

· · · · · · · · · · · · · · · ·

MAPLE SUGARING is a New England icon. Galvanized buckets hanging from trees above snow-covered ground and rising steam from an evaporator are among the most enduring, endearing, and engaging images of the region. A substantial amount of syrup is produced in other states, and by far most comes from Canada, but in the public mind New England is the maple capital. The following pages explore why.

Sugaring highlights and fosters a surprisingly wide range of classic New England characteristics. Among them are respect for deep history, Yankee ingenuity, connection to nature, affection for rural simplicity, sustainability, a strong work ethic, determination to prevail, hope for the future, savvy marketing, self-reliance, coping with variable weather, and delighting in homey foods. And while much nostalgia and some hyperbole are embedded in such attributes, they also remain remarkably viable. They are qualities from which readers in all walks of life and living anywhere in the world can draw inspiration.

There are many fine books on maple sugaring. Most of them are histories, personal chronicles, or about how to make syrup. This volume is not a history, a memoir, or a guide to producing a product. It partakes of some of these features, but more than detailing the past, the routines of sugaring, and the process of making syrup, I try to capture, however imperfectly, the indomitable spirit of those who tap and boil sap. Through my own experiences making syrup and the lively stories of many sugarmakers throughout the six New England states, I examine the sugaring way of life. I wanted to know what inflamed the passion of sugarmakers despite the hard work, yearly gamble with the weather, and other challenges.

Through the eyes of those who make syrup, scientists, government officials, equipment dealers and manufacturers, educators, and others, this book looks at community and family life, the advance of technology, heritage values, innovative products and nutrition, environmental issues like climate change and invasive species, marketing, the joy of trees and forests, agriculture as entertainment, and other matters. Doing so paints an impressionist-like picture of a landscape and its people.

Few activities so tightly bind culture and nature as maple sugaring. Rarely does an undertaking fuse the individuals involved so perfectly with the territory in which they live. With necessary conditions limited to a small corner of the planet, maple syrup is a true marker of place.

So long as sugarmakers inspire curious people to tap trees in their backyards or down the street, and children of all ages stand wide-eyed watching sap boil, maple syrup will embody the essence of New England. Join me discovering a labor of materiality and myth, space and time, muscle and soil, sweat and sweetness. New horizons beckon from a time-honored process.

Maple Sugaring

Maple Passion

"IS IT REAL MAPLE SYRUP?" That's my first question in an unfamiliar restaurant when I order pancakes, perhaps with a side of bacon and a couple of bull's-eye eggs. Not long ago, I perched myself on a stool in a silvery train-car-style eastern Massachusetts diner circa 1950 where the menu promised old-fashioned, home-style blueberry waffles. Perhaps not as good as what I could make in my own kitchen, but I was away from home and hungry. Besides, where better to have old-timey comfort food than a venerable eatery with gleaming stainless accents and terrazzo floors. "For an extra buck you get maple made just a few miles away in the next town. Otherwise it's the fake stuff—Aunt Jemima, I think," the ponytailed waitress said. I was glad to spend a little more. Otherwise it would have been an omelet and home fries.

Despite the region's long association with maple sugaring, even here in New England you have to ask if it's the real deal, because some cost-conscious restaurants don't serve it. If you've grown up on maple syrup or acquired the taste later in life, you can't stomach so-called "table" or "pancake" syrup. They may advertise maple flavor, depict quaint cabins on their label, or have "Vermont" in their name, but they are viscous, cloying, and have a manufactured aftertaste. Maple syrup is made from the pure, clear sap of maple trees. While table or pancake syrups are not made from tables or flapjacks, as the names seem to suggest, they are generally concocted from corn syrup and may use sodium benzoate, cellulose gum, and artificial flavor with propylene glycol, sulfites, and dextrose. Used to be that sometimes a minuscule amount of actual maple syrup was added, but that seems largely a thing of the past. Sure, real maple syrup is a bit pricey, but when you discover the labor that goes into making it, it's a bargain. I spent more than a decade of frenetic days, long nights, sweat and aching muscles finding out by running a small sugarhouse in the old mill village of Collinsville, Connecticut, once a world capital of axe and machete manufacture.

A couple of tablespoons or so of golden syrup hardly seemed sufficient when drizzled over my goodly stack of waffles punctuated with dark-blue fruity dots, but I poured it gingerly over the crispy grid of squares, knowing what little I was using took about a quart and a half of sap to create. Like in gold mining, where tons of rock are crushed, sifted, and treated to produce a few ounces of precious metal, a sugarmaker gathers large quantities of sap and by boiling and other clever innovations drives off the water and concentrates the sugar. Maple syrup is nothing more than condensed maple sap. The only added ingredient—leaving no taste, color, or odor—is the sugarmaker's considerable labor. And usually that labor is itself the producer's principal reward, for few earn much cash at it. Only a tiny percentage of big sugarmakers using thousands or even tens of thousands of taps will make a good living. The vast majority, hobbyists and small operators, make little or no money.

In spite of sugaring's demanding bull work that might harden and obscure metaphysical notions, sugarmakers are a remarkably philosophic group. Regardless of the number of taps or size of the evaporator, sugaring is a seasonal rite of passage, a species of secular religion attaching a person to the larger cycles and rhythms of nature and life. Sugarmakers describe it as an addiction, a fever, even a contagious disease. It's easy to get hooked, almost impossible to stop. Getting a few dollars for their work is rewarding, but for most producers it's not their principal motivation.

"You can be successful at any size," says maple impresario Bruce Bascom of New Hampshire, one of the nation's largest producers, packers, wholesalers, and equipment dealers; "it just depends on what you want to get out of it." As with a vegetable garden, a person can grow a few tomatoes and cucumbers, plant corn and rows of radishes sufficient for his family and a few friends, or can expand enough for sales at a roadside stand or get even bigger and wholesale the crop.

One tap or a hundred thousand, sugaring can be a life-changing experience.

Backyard sugaring remains a time-honored activity that can stay homebound and close-knit or grow into a large company. With a season that lasts only about six weeks, maple lends itself to the devoted amateur, demonstrating that the passions of our free time are not necessarily frivolous, but can represent the best in dedication and craftsmanship. "It can be brutally hard work and the hours beyond exhausting," Bascom told me, "but the sap run is short enough to withstand." Until the advent of new technologies in the 1980s making large quantities easier to process, it was almost always part-time, something that dairy and other farmers did to make a few dollars in mud season so they could buy seed and other necessities. To this day, only a relatively few are in the maple business year-round.

∘ ∘ ∘ ∘ ∘ ∘ ∘

A NEIGHBOR'S ancient sugar maple crashing to the ground in a violent autumn windstorm over twenty-five years ago began my education as a syrup maker. She missed summer shade, splashy fall color, and the tree's muscular winter limbs, but most of all she longed for the sap. Partially heating her house by woodstove, she used to keep a pot of sap simmering on the hot cast iron to moisten the dry interior air. The dark syrup obtained as a by-product had a slightly burnt flavor, but made at home, it was the best she had ever tasted.

The next February she asked permission to tap the two large maples that then stood like pillars on either side of my front walk. I watched in fascination as white wood spooled from holes drilled with a carpenter's brace. Using a small hammer, she lightly tapped galvanized spiles into the openings and then attached a couple of gallon milk containers using picture-frame wire. Every few seconds a drop of clear liquid fell into the jugs with a heartbeat-like pulse. I was mesmerized.

I became as devoted as a daily soap opera fan to watching the containers, and they quickly superseded my bird feeders as objects of out-the-window interest and a measure of the changing season. My glances through the glass became an obsession, and even when I was out of the house my mind was drawn back to the trees. Warmer, sunnier days meant a continuous dribble, but when the temperature did not get much above freezing or the sky was overcast, drips were slow and far between. Nothing happened on cold days, and it made me anxious. I began describing the weather not by the usual conventions of cracker-barrel forecasters and meteorologists but by the amount of sap and frequency of drops, as if they were as probative as a changing barometer or cloud formations. I was hooked.

The following year, I put in four taps of my own and boiled sap on my kitchen stove, burning one pot, curling a few pieces of already loose wallpaper, and producing almost a pint of thin, cloudy, but tasty dark syrup. Next season, I bought the most powerful twin hot plate my hardware store could find and boiled in my garage, far from any wallpaper. With my backyard and neighbor's trees recruited for the cause, I had eight taps and made almost a half gallon of the golden liquid, which I bottled in half-pint mason jars and gifted to smiles and rave reviews.

No twelve-step program for me. Not even a twelve-tap program. I was a confirmed maple-oholic. I made a pilgrimage to the sugarhouse of Rob Lamothe, a genial, bearded Pied Piper of sugaring in the next town with a growing family operation and a brisk equipment business. Rob didn't have to give a sales pitch. His generosity sharing knowledge and natural enthusiasm for an activity he loved were infectious. Securing permission from more neighbors to tap trees, I tossed my milk jugs and bought the traditional sixteen-quart galvanized buckets and a barrel evaporator—a horizontal thirty-five-gallon drum set on legs so it could be used like a woodstove. It was fitted with a flat-bottom pan on top in which to boil sap. I had twenty-one taps and made five gallons of syrup.

The next year, I received permission to use the trees at both the Congregational church down the street and the phone company, whose nearby switching station had a maple out front. I had thirty-four taps. The season after that, I visited Rob just as he returned from his ancestral Quebec with a load of new and used equipment. I purchased a small two-by-four-foot professional-style evaporator. It had twin stainless-steel pans that separated fresh sap from nearly finished syrup, thereby providing continuous flow of the transforming liquid.

I bought a 150-gallon storage tank, a hydrometer for measuring the density of syrup, a grading kit, and plastic jugs just like the big guys used for their product. Eventually, I had over eighty taps along the streets and in the yards of homes and businesses throughout the small downtown where I live within sight of town hall.

Sugaring captured my imagination, was a lifestyle, became part of my identity. I defined the years by the sugaring weather, the sweetness of sap, and the amount of syrup I produced. I met other sugarmakers, went to maple meetings, and was eventually elected to the board of the Maple Syrup Producers Association of Connecticut. There was excitement in the way sugarmakers always looked forward to the future, the grand gamble with Mother Nature and new technologies and products. The wisdom of a deep heritage shared with old-timers tempered innovation and kept cultural amnesia at bay. They might grumble about adverse weather, new government regulations, and the cost of replacement equipment, but their complaints were always softened with a joy in producing something natural that simply made people happy. I had dreams of expanding my somewhat urban experiment in agriculture, though I stopped short of installing tubing, which would have had to be exceedingly high or tie up traffic. Still, it would have been fun to have those colorful hollow ribbons of plastic strung around the village and sparkling in the sunlight.

I was making just over fifty gallons of syrup in a good year, which means I was hauling and boiling about two thousand gallons of sap. It was backbreaking work, but I was energized by it, totally in thrall until my vertebrae literally gave out. Despite two surgeries to repair the damage and help from my children and neighbors collecting and boiling sap, I was finally forced to stop sugaring.

Though it has been over ten years since I made syrup, I still get the itch and longing in late winter when daylight grows and temperatures regularly climb above freezing. I feel like a baseball fan as Grapefruit League games approach or a fisherman awaiting opening day. Spring is less about colorful flowers and the smell of softening soil than the aroma of wood smoke mixed with sweet steam.

During the season, I drive around to see who is tapping and where. Unless I do so, I feel a hunger, an emptiness that no number of waffles smothered in syrup can satisfy. I stop into sugarhouses to chat and smell the mapley moist warmth of these New England saunas where there is always a welcome, some equipment to be tinkered with, and a few stories to be shared. I found that you can stop boiling sap, but never quite quit being a sugarmaker once it's in your blood.

* * * * * * *

SUGAR MAKING is ancient, simple, yet somehow mysterious. A familiar homegrown local food in my corner of the world, it nevertheless seems exotic, the transformation from sap to syrup almost magical. It's part art, alchemy, and science. Though looking at a liquid boil is not much more exciting than the proverbial opportunity of watching paint dry, sugaring not only addicts sugarmakers but intrigues everyone from grammar schoolers to octogenarians, thousands of whom are drawn yearly to visit sugarhouses and watch the process. Perhaps our fascination has something to do with our love of sweets, our nostalgia for simpler times, hunger for healthful and pure foods, or that this first crop of the new year takes us from frigid winter to the threshold of spring and yields a golden, luminescent liquid that seems the very distillation of sunshine itself.

Maple sugaring may be the most Yankee of Yankee activities. On one hand, it has an old-timey backwoods image, but shrewdly uses high-tech equipment like reverse osmosis, vacuum pumps, and check-valve spiles. There's a dirt-road, country-store sales pitch, yet sophisticated marketing sells not just a product but an experience, a sense of place and time. If it's true that we are what we eat, maple syrup has an edgy difference. With rare exception, it's a food harvested not from plantations, but wild-grown forests. These are managed to favor the sweet trees by people serious about long-term, sustainable stewardship of the woods. Maple is at the confluence of wild nature and culture, a hunter-gatherer activity that's become somewhat domesticated. This connection to ancient food harvesting may be part of the magic.

Maple syrup is a true marker of place, a symbol of authenticity and deep heritage that is produced in one region of the world. Though in the United States it's primarily a product of the Northeast and upper Midwest, sugaring can be a lens focusing on and illuminating a wide swath of America's cultural geography. It's a story of entrepreneur-

The most Yankee of Yankee activities

ship, technical innovation, family life, and our relationship to nature. Its history is rooted in Native American traditions and the politics of national independence and the antislavery movement. Nevertheless, maple issues are as contemporary as the economics of international trade. Sugaring is sensitive to environmental change from invasive species, air pollution, and global warming; some observers believe that sugarmakers may be the canary in the coal mine for such environmental transformations. Recently, maple has become emblematic of increasing interest in independent lifestyles and healthful food choices.

In the United States, commercial sugaring regions extend south to Virginia's mountains and as far west as Minnesota. But for generations Canada has produced the vast majority of maple syrup, with the province of Quebec making close to 80 percent of the world's total. A syrup cartel, the Federation of Quebec Maple Syrup Producers, tightly regulates marketing and production in our northern neighbor. With a strategic reserve, or surplus, of tens of millions of pounds of syrup, it not only controls the wholesale price in Canada, but largely in this country as well. Though sometimes pejoratively referred to as the OPEC of syrup, with a barrel of the sweet stuff commanding a price much higher than the standard West Texas Intermediate crude, even American producers acknowledge that the federation has beneficially stabilized prices in a business otherwise subject to wide supply and price swings from the vicissitudes of weather.

With production in good years at well over a million gallons, Vermont is by far the leading syrup producer in the United States, usually making twice as much as its closest rival, New York, and generally two times what the other five New England states produce combined. Certainly, in the public mind Vermont is the place most intimately and immediately identified with syrup, and the state has long been a leader in research, regulation, and inspection. Fortunately, Vermont's stature in the maple world has, to some degree, radiated by association to the other New England states. While New England is not the big player on the world maple stage, it is a place where the sugaring culture reaches its apotheosis, looming larger than what is revealed by mere measurements in gallons of syrup or trees tapped.

Maple sugaring exemplifies the classic New England values of connectedness to land and community, Yankee ingenuity, observation of the natural world, heritage pride, entrepreneurship, homespun hospitality, make-do and can-do, and simplicity. If you want to understand much of present-day America in a grounded, tangible, and fundamental way, sugaring is a palpable means. Just as the nineteenth-century New England transcendentalists like Ralph Waldo Emerson and Henry David Thoreau found universal truths in the details of particulars, so too can larger truths about America be wrested from the sugaring culture of this region.

Sugaring simultaneously keeps alive both the old and contemporary New England, whether in the shadow of Hartford office towers or the most rural precincts of Maine. It's not a "Bert and I" story, a *Yankee* magazine puff piece, and it doesn't look like an advertisement for Pepperidge Farm. The much-vaunted and lamented New England character is not dying. It's present in the sugarmakers who each year return to their evaporators like migratory birds. They remind us that the essence of a region is not just in what we see, however careful our observations. It's in the doing of something that binds people to a place where they are firmly rooted in the here-and-now while simultaneously able to reach back to deeper connections.

America needs maple syrup. Not so much to drench its pancakes to satisfy an insatiable sweet tooth, but to tell us who we are, where we've been, and where we might be going. It ties the past to the present and the present to the future. It's a small world that reveals something larger and more fundamental, like a hilltop sugarbush offering a distant view.

Maple Dip

Yield: 2 cups

INGREDIENTS

8 ounces cream cheese, softened
1 cup pure maple sugar
1 teaspoon vanilla extract
Fresh fruit slices, such as apple, pineapple, banana, peach, or pear

DIRECTIONS

1. Combine cream cheese, maple sugar, and vanilla extract in a bowl; mix until smooth.
2. Chill in refrigerator until ready to serve.
3. Spoon into serving bowl and serve with the fresh fruit slices.

Recipe by Wenzel Sugarhouse

Butternut Squash / Maple Soup

Yield: 8 servings

INGREDIENTS

2 ounces butter
2 cups chopped onion
1 tablespoon cornstarch
4 cups chicken stock
3 pounds cooked, mashed
  butternut squash

Salt and pepper to taste
¾ cup half-and-half (or cream)
⅓ cup maple syrup
Toppings for serving

DIRECTIONS

1. In a large skillet or kettle, melt the butter and sauté the onions for about 3 minutes, until translucent.
2. Sprinkle the onions with the cornstarch and mix thoroughly. Cook until absorbed.
3. Add the chicken stock a little at a time and cook, stirring frequently, until the liquid starts to thicken.
4. Add the squash, mixing as you add. Bring to a boil, then simmer for 15 minutes. Stir often so it doesn't stick.
5. Purée a portion at a time in a blender or food processor, or use an immersion blender.
6. Return to cooking pot and add the half-and-half (or cream) and the Connecticut maple syrup, mixing well. Let simmer on medium low heat until heated through.
7. Serve immediately, or keep in refrigerator for up to 2 days.

You can top the soup with minced parsley, thyme, rosemary, nutmeg, cinnamon, sour cream, or nuts, depending on your taste. Feel free to experiment with a selection of different toppings each time!

Recipe by Kay Carroll

Time, Space, and
····· the Special Theory of ·····
Maple Relativity

IT'S ROUGHLY AROUND the middle of January that sugarmakers, even retired ones like me, become vigilant about weather. We don't necessarily pay attention to the forecasts of professionally cheerful meteorological evangelists with their Doppler radar and satellite data. We notice the small local details visible from the doorway or sensed during a walk down the street or a hike in the woods: the temperature, amount and intensity of sunlight, the cloud cover. If the old saying that "when the wind's from the west the sap runs best" can be believed, we notice the direction of the breeze. We become hyperaware and somewhat obsessive as we get psyched to tap. Tapping day is the ribbon-cutting on a new season, a portent like the first robin snatching a worm from the lawn.

Since maple sap runs with the fluctuation of daytime thaws and nighttime freezes, traditional sugarmakers using buckets have usually tapped in late winter at the outset of the first stretch of sunny weather when thermometers rise to about forty degrees Fahrenheit. But like most everything about sugaring, tapping time is a wager with Mother Nature. A sugarmaker's rabid weather watching creates a pressurized excitement, and with all the anticipation it's easy to tap prematurely and get a small run of sap lasting only a day or two. It might not even be enough to make boiling worthwhile. You can find your storage tank clogged with a solid block of sap ice and the trees locked in a cold snap and refusing to yield a drop more.

In parts of southern New England, Lincoln's February 12 birthday has been the cue. Vermont sugarmakers customarily waited until after town meeting day, the first Tuesday of March. Years ago, according to some old-timers, a farmer might base his number of taps on how much he had to pay in taxes following passage of the local budget. But the calendar and political events are useless. The sugaring world sculpts and bends time in a unique way that belies the orderly mechanics of any clock. Whether it's tapping, sap flow, evaporating, or bottling, sugaring's compressed season distorts the progress of hours, speeding them to a frenetic pace or slowing them to a glacial crawl in an Einstein-like warp of normal experience.

Sure, it's a crazy big leap, but if Albert Einstein had been a sugar-maker, the experience might have induced him to propose his theory of special relativity earlier, sooner consigning concepts of absolute motion to the trash heap of ideas. In the early twentieth century, around the time the Cary Maple Sugar Company of St. Johnsbury, Vermont, became the world's largest maple products wholesaler and the U.S. Pure Food and Drug Act outlawed syrup adulteration, Einstein postulated movement as a relative measurement between frames of reference, replacing distinctions between space and time with a four-dimensional continuum called space-time. Though destined for much more lofty purposes, the great scientist's theory also illuminates the way in which sugarmakers experience time, as well as the deep intimacy between location and seasonal movement that is a hallmark of sugaring, seemingly fusing time and place into a single phenomenon.

Few sugarmakers are likely to be impressed by such theories. Those with even a modicum of experience have a sixth sense about when to tap, like gamblers knowing when to play their hand and when to fold. It's nature's casino, and you take your chances. Of course, with innovations like tubing, high-tech taps, and vacuum pumps that suck sap from a tree, dried-out tapholes from early tapping is not so much of an issue anymore. Besides, big sugarmakers with thousands of holes to drill need days or weeks to get the job done, even with many hands using speedy electric drills. They have no choice but to tap into frozen trunks long before they begin to drip.

• • • • • • •

IT'S THE SMALL-TIMERS with buckets, like sugarmakers past, who still tap on sunny days of soft air after weeks of frigid temperatures. Smells are again on the breeze, and the steepening angle of the sun warms the nape of the neck. With no more than eighty taps, I had the luxury of drilling the holes myself, using a hand-powered carpenter's brace fitted with a seven-sixteenths-inch bit (though now five-sixteenths are used with smaller spouts, with no appreciable reduction in sap flow). The holes were no more than two inches deep at a slight upward angle into light-colored, healthy wood. Since previous tapholes should be eight to twelve inches distant vertically and at least an inch horizontally to avoid wood no longer conducive to sap flow, I always gave the trunk a quick inspection. I got to know each individual maple better, recalling past seasons by finding completely healed tapholes that left marks like "outie" belly buttons, and gauging the tree's health by how quickly last year's holes had filled.

I tended to tap in late morning when snowmelt was echoing in gutters and tinkling into catch basins along the street in my village sugarbush of roadside and backyard trees. At the base of some trunks there might be a little mud pooled on the sunny side. As I drilled, curls of blond wood wound along the bit and fell to the ground. Once the bit was withdrawn, sap would dribble out, followed by a regular pulse of drops whose frequency depended not just on the weather but perhaps the location of the taphole relative to the sun or a big root. I'd gently bang in the metal spout and hang my bucket to the reassuringly regular ping of liquid dropping to the bottom. Ah, the joy of instant gratification.

Most sugarmakers spend such days in the woods, enjoying the sound of wind and creaking trees, chickadees and other birds between the short-lived whine of a cordless drill used in tapping. Depending on cold and depth of snow, it can be both strenuous and peaceful. Sometimes the work is accomplished on snowshoes. But because my sugarbush was in the center of a small town, on tapping day I gave up the serenity of the woods for serendipitous conversations with neighbors. Long before anyone was sitting on a porch, attending outdoor concerts, or slowly strolling the sidewalks, I got caught up on who had had the flu, the neighbor kids' grades, the quality of the ski season, who had bought a new car, and what was planned for the garden. A harbinger of warmer weather, I was a sight glad to be seen, and my hanging buckets on the trees was an occasion for cheer, a mark of optimism that spring would soon arrive. Needless to say, time expanded relative to the number of people I ran into and the length of conversations. The hours spent tapping had less to do with how long it took to drill a hole and hang a bucket than whom I might meet and the urgency of the conversation. Again, I was caught in Einstein's theoretical grip.

Though there have been dramatic innovations in production since Native American times, perhaps most in the past generation, sugaring has long remained a process of tapping trees, collecting sap, concentrating the sweet by removing water, putting the finished syrup into containers, and distributing it. Afterward, there's lots of cleaning, repairs, and, if you use wood fuel, cutting and stacking.

With sap running at the whim of the weather and often responding to micro-conditions not predicted on the morning forecast, collecting it injects a delightful if annoying unpredictability into a world increasingly regulated by alarms and notices where we are regimented with fairly precise routines of work, appointments, meetings, and even recreation planned weeks and months in advance. While a sugarmaker can, to a limited extent, plan when to boil, filter, or can syrup, sap collection is almost completely unpredictable and requires immediate attention. A bucket or tank running over is as demanding as a nagging two-year-old. It feels like money dropping through a hole in your pocket.

On sunny weekend afternoons, collecting sap was fun. Like tapping day, it became a social event. I'd run into neighbors asking about the progress of the season, putting in their syrup orders, spilling a little gossip, or urging me to come to a town meeting or the high school play. As we talked, I lifted galvanized buckets off a tree, poured them into five-gallon pails, and carried the pails to a plastic tank in the back of my pickup. Sometimes a neighbor would join me, riding shotgun and helping empty the buckets, providing more warmth with friendship than a February sun at noon might offer. Time seemed to fly.

Approaching the trees and gazing into their crowns occasioned a kind of interspecies intimacy. I was visiting with old friends. Each maple almost seemed to have a different personality expressed in its size and shape, the amount of sap it yielded, and how it responded to particular kinds of weather. Sugarmakers who have gone from buckets

A sign of winter winding down

to tubing have few regrets, except maybe when an ice storm turns their lines into a tangle, but they frequently miss knowing their trees as individuals.

Despite my sylvan affections and sense of camaraderie, the trees never ran at my convenience. I'd get antsy finding myself trapped in meetings that seemed to go on forever at my Hartford office and was unable to concentrate on work during days awash with sunshine when the mercury flirted with fifty degrees. I'd imagine drops so fast that they were almost a stream, buckets overflowing, sap puddling around the roots. The trees had no regard for my overscheduled life filled with a job, children, home repairs, errands, and the occasional dinner and movie out. Often I'd find myself half exhausted, collecting late at night or before dawn. Sometimes it was urgent, as when the temperature was plummeting rapidly and sap might freeze solid in the buckets, causing them damage and leaving little room for the next run. I ventured out in wind-whipped rain and snowstorms, finding my slicker and Bean boots more valuable than my best suit. My fingers froze and my back ached, but the trees were relentless. Toward the end of the season, I'd walk around dizzily in zombie-like depletion and chain-suck cough drops in a vain attempt to keep a cold at bay. The trees kept their own secret schedules, maintained their own measures of time.

When conditions were right, my maples poured gallons to my delight, and irritation at being a slave to their caprice faded. The pace became frenetic. Then temperatures would dip for a few days or even a week or more. I'd quickly recover my sleep and equanimity and find myself eager for the next run. The trees were teasing me. I became fidgety and dull with waiting. I remembered seventh-generation Vermont sugarmaker Burr Morse's quip that maple people "are more than fussy—we're downright neurotic."

Collecting sap did not end with visiting the trees and emptying the gathering pails into my truck. I needed a place to store all that liquid until ready to boil. In my first two seasons, I underestimated how much the trees could yield on a warm day, and after filling the plastic barrel, pails, and carboys I'd procured for the purpose, I began using soda and milk bottles destined for recycling and then frantically filling my kitchen pots until I had to borrow a saucepan from my neighbor to cook dinner.

By the third year I'd wised up. I hauled the sap back to my garage-turned-sugarhouse and backed the truck up the long driveway. With a submersible pump in the collection tank, I sucked the liquid up to a larger tank elevated on a stand made of rusting tubular scrap steel and angle iron leaning against the north side of the sugarhouse. Here it would be mostly in shadow, keeping the sap cool and fresh until ready to boil. A valve-controlled pipe led from the tank to the evaporator.

At first I had a plywood-covered, oblong galvanized stock tank that had once slaked the thirst of cows or sheep. Later I bought a 250-gallon food-grade plastic tank, a necessity in these days of increasing concern for product purity. It took several minutes to pump the sap, but it felt like hours in cold or raw weather late at night. Lastly, I rinsed out the collection tank and flushed the hose and pump, a dull and solitary job. By late in the season my reddened and chapped hands let me know they'd had enough drudgery.

Collecting with buckets is a lot of work, and sugarmakers of any size now use tubing. But regardless of the sap-gathering method, the sugaring paradox is that the next step is to rid yourself of most of what you've worked so hard to accumulate. Sap is mostly water, typically ranging from 1.5 to 3 percent sugar. In order to get a gallon of proper density syrup from 2 percent sap, roughly 43.5 gallons are required. At 2.2 percent, just over 39.5 gallons are needed, and for the very rare tree that has 10 percent sugar, only about 8.7 gallons.

Ice and fire are the time-honored ways of concentrating sugar. After a frigid night, sugarmakers often toss away the ice in a storage tank or bucket of sap because liquids with less sugar freeze first, leaving the remainder more concentrated. Though long utilized, this is a small gesture toward producing syrup. Boiling has always been the mainstay of sugaring as far back as Native Americans, who placed hot rocks into containers of sap to drive off the water. Boiling is still necessary to achieve maple flavor and color, though today larger sugarmakers first extract much of the water through reverse osmosis—RO, in sugaring shorthand—a process adapted from desalinization technology, whereby the sap is pushed through a membrane that allows water to pass but not larger sugar molecules.

In dawn's dim gloaming, or after a long day at work, I'd lift the overhead door of what looked like an ordinary garage. Flicking on a bare incandescent bulb revealed the enchanted space of the sugarhouse. There among buckets and various other containers, tangled hoses, a splitting maul, and the other tackle of small-time sugar making, I'd kneel before the cast-iron doors of the firebox, called an arch, light a nest of paper and kindling, and watch the flames begin to dance. Soon I could feel uneven warmth on my face. Along the wall, the blaze cast shadows on the lawn mower, garden tools, and children's bicycles that seemed to have been hibernating since fall. This plain space for the equipage of suburban life seemed momentarily transformed to a wizard's lair of alchemy where what looked like water would soon be transformed, if not into wine, at least into a kind of liquid gold. Expanding with the heat, the stainless-steel pan startled me with irregular pings. I slammed the cast-iron doors and got busy.

I opened valves on the white PVC sap line that ran from the outside storage tank through the wall and across the sugarhouse to a rectangular galvanized container, like a loaf pan, resting on top of the back of the evaporator, where rising steam would warm the fresh sap before it dripped through yet another valve into the boil below. I made sure there was enough sap in the back of the evaporator pan where the stainless was formed into corrugated channels, called flues, giving the fire more surface area so the clear liquid would boil faster. The front pan, where denser, more sugary pre-syrup flowed, was flat so it would boil more slowly, since sugary liquids can quickly caramelize and burn, destroying not only the syrup, but often the pan. I adjusted the valve that regulated flow from the back to the front pan and stepped outside to split a few chunks of wood.

Pin-prick bubbles formed in the pan, and I heard slight rumbles as the vaguest wisps of steam began to rise like mist off a chilling pond in autumn. Opening the firebox, I tossed in a couple more pieces of wood and listened to a low roar like dragon breath as the hungry flames sucked in oxygen. Jerkily moving like a butterfly from flower to flower, I played with the valves, prepared the next charge of wood for the fire, tested the more viscous liquid with a scoop to estimate its density, and readied cone-shaped felt filters suspended over a bucket for my first draw-off of nearly finished product. Thumbprint swirls of heat in the pan soon turned to churning bubbles and then to large cauliflower-like upheavals. Steam hung in the sugarhouse like fog before rising out a skylight in cumulous puffs. It was a day of clear sky and high pressure when the sap seemed eager to boil and time moved quickly.

. . . .

THE SWEET VAPOR of a boil is intoxicating. The muscle rhythm of stoking the fire, adjusting the flow of sap, and drawing off finished syrup is hypnotic. The smell, the moist warmth, and the sound of boiling and dripping produce a sugarmaker's high—a kind of sensory joy forged in hard work and the pleasure of making something natural and nourishing.

Rising steam is also a welcome-mat for company. While a sugarmaker is always puttering around his evaporator, once a steady boil has begun there is plenty of time. In fact, boiling sap can be said to be made of time—minutes, hours, sometimes days. It's not just time for processing a food—it's time for visitors who work in offices and retail shops or whose jobs are focused on computers or carpentry to share in something attached to natural cycles and a deep heritage whose simplicity never fails to intrigue. They become part of something elemental and feel good about it. Describing his sugarhouse as second only to a general store as a gathering place, Burr Morse calls it a "focal point for pointless jabber and sweet triviality." Time in a sugarhouse speeds up with visitors, and slows almost painfully when you're alone. Sugaring not only produces syrup—the time it takes also generates stories.

Although a passerby once dialed 911 because he thought the steam was smoke and my garage aflame, the guys at the firehouse knew better, and a phone call to me kept the sirens silent. But since they were together anyway, they came by in a pumper to satisfy their sweet tooths with samples right off the evaporator. We swapped a few lies and had some laughs at the caller's expense.

Like the pulse of sap, the flow of visitors is unpredictable. They come in dribs and drabs and occasionally in a steady stream. Sometimes I could go for hours on a sunny weekend and not only run the evaporator without interruption, but get through the paper and several magazines that had been waiting months on my bedside table. Other times, I'd be startled from a late-night fugue by a friend I thought had hit the pillow hours ago. It was an ongoing open house requiring no invitation, and the number of guests was yet another measure of time.

I liked it best when children came by and would stare moon-eyed into the steam as if they'd entered a fairy's lair. Sometimes they would arrive with parents nervously working like sheepdogs to keep them from the hot arch or tripping on an errant bucket or hose. Older ones would bicycle over on warmer days. At the bank or the barber they might be treated to a lollipop or some candy around Halloween, but a paper thimble of near-syrup right off the evaporator was a wonder-working potion. Whenever there was fresh snow, they'd eagerly collect a bowlful and gasp as I'd drizzle hot syrup over it, creating maple taffy before their eyes. Often on weekend afternoons the sugarhouse would be filled with the screeching chirp and shout of children.

"We're drinking tree blood!" some third-grader would inevitably shout. Empathic kids, perhaps recalling a vaccination, sometimes asked if the drill hurt the trees. Older ones would eagerly help collect sap, though between spillage and a few drinks I'd have been better off without their labor. Nevertheless, their puppy-like enthusiasm was a bigger payday than I ever got from a gallon of syrup. Familiar with the process, my own kids and those of my neighbors would turn into mini tour guides, and I cringed to hear my own words and intonations echoed in their squeaky voices.

Living two blocks up the hill, my buddy Alan was a frequent visitor to the sugarhouse, where, like Thoreau, I kept three chairs on sabbatical from the summer terrace—one for myself, a second for company, and a third for society. He'd see steam rising, come in without a knock, plop down in one of the plastic-webbed seats, and pick up the newspaper with little more than a taciturn "hello." After he'd digested a few column inches, we'd be off discussing Middle East politics, the power company rate increase, or some nearby mayor charged with corruption. His blood churning with the news, he'd get up and stretch, lean over the evaporator and breathe the steam like a person with a cold savoring a vaporizer.

At such times, my fire department friend Bill and his wife Teri might be passing by on one of their long walks, and we'd catch up about our kids or the latest fitting or hose lay on one of the trucks down at the firehouse. I'd be adjusting the flow of sap into the back pan or turning the draw-off valve and pouring syrup into a cone filter to remove niter, inert sand-like minerals that precipitate out of boiled sap. We'd chat while I moved about the machine, and the conversation might morph into a discussion of the town budget or an impending snowstorm.

The sugarhouse had the natural conviviality and easy talk of a neighborhood tavern or coffee shop, where you never knew who'd pop in or where the conversation might lead. Sometimes an impromptu party might erupt when someone came by with a few beers or cups of coffee. Toward the end of the season, when the last, usually very dark syrup was for my own consumption, I'd sometimes boil hot dogs in the slightly sweet back pan while talk turned to the new baseball season.

Some of the deepest conversations I've ever had occurred while I boiled into the wee hours when a friend or neighbor who tossed and turned with troubled sleep came by under the silence of stars. There were problems on their mind and no one to talk to past midnight unless they saw my light and rising steam. The visit might be generated by an argument with a spouse, fears about a teenager on drugs, or a sick parent barely clinging to reality and life. Perhaps it was the mesmerizing pulse of the boil or soothing sweetness of the steam, but personal details I'd never hear in daylight came spilling out. Maybe there was something insular and comforting about the sugarhouse, brightly lit, warm and moist in the icy dark. They could stare at the boil while they spilled their guts. I fussed about the evaporator, something to fill the silences and keep us from the awkward tension of constant eye contact.

Once a mere acquaintance nearing forty came by to tell me a sheriff had served divorce papers that afternoon. He leaned over the evaporator and began sobbing, perhaps hoping the moisture would mask his tears. He'd been unfaithful, and his wife would not accept his apologies and promises. Another time, a friend had gotten a late-night call about the death of her mother. Distraught and shaking, she didn't want to awaken anyone and so drove more than five miles to see if I was boiling. There was always a powerful but brief intimacy, and I got to know a handful of people in dimensions few saw. Of course, it was an ephemeral closeness, because like the old saw about Las Vegas, what was said in the sugarhouse stayed there.

Among the most electric moments in the season were the three or four times I'd pack syrup into containers. I'd rewarm it on the stove in my kitchen or, in subsequent years, in a separate boxy stainless container heated with propane and made for the purpose. The room would fill with maple smell as the syrup reached the right tempera- ture. I'd filter again and test the density with a hydrometer. I'd taste it, check the color, and ladle the hot, golden liquid into plastic jugs or log cabin-shaped tins, screw on the caps, and turn them upside down to seal as they cooled. I'd recruit my kids and friends to help. A glow of satisfaction overtook me as the last step in production was completed and the secret of how much syrup the year would yield was revealed quart by quart, pint by pint. Each bottle seemed a notch in time. The counter, floors, and equipment grew sticky as the process wore on, and the last job of a long day was washing down.

Toward the end of the season, when there was no threat of sap re- freezing in the buckets, I'd often be collecting late at night to ensure I got the full day's run. Where once I was bundled in a coat and thick gloves, I now worked in shirtsleeves. In a fog of sublimating snow and squishy muddy ground, I'd go out with a flashlight to check for moths, ants, or other spring-awakening creatures that might land in a bucket. Some of the sap could be cloudy from bacteria on a warm day, or might have turned as yellow as urine and bitter after buds opened on the tree's branches, heralding the season's end. My last few collections were to the otherworldly sleigh-bell-like sounds of spring peepers who called from a nearby swamp. This last "frog run" of sap produced the darkest, strongest-flavored syrup, my favorite.

Sometimes I sugared into the first week of April, but usually the season ended in late March. On a sunny day I'd pull my spouts with a soft hammer tap and toss the buckets into the back of my pickup. Ending the season was sad, but I was eager to have my schedule back and no longer abandon my life to the vagaries of weather and sap flow.

Of course, the season wasn't over when it was over, because all the buckets, pails, taps, storage tanks, hoses, valves, and tools had to be sanitized and put away. The evaporator had to be scrubbed, including the build-up of carbon beneath the pan from a season of fires. Usu- ally it was a day when sun beat down on my driveway and I'd wash everything with a bleach solution and triple rinse. About five car lengths long, my driveway that day parked tens of galvanized buckets. It was pure drudgery, and I usually recruited Alan and sometimes my preteen son to help. I saw it as compensation for the comfort of the sugarhouse. Lastly, everything had to be packed carefully away like Christmas decorations awaiting the next season.

Carrot-Ginger-Maple Soup

Yield: 8–10 servings

INGREDIENTS

2 tablespoons extra-virgin olive oil
2 large onions, diced
1 clove garlic, minced
6 large carrots, peeled, cut into 1-inch lengths
4 large potatoes, peeled, diced
1½-inch piece of gingerroot, peeled, shaved*
9 cups chicken or vegetable stock (more or less as needed)
½ teaspoon salt or to taste
½ teaspoon pepper or to taste
⅓ cup maple syrup
Garnish, for serving*

DIRECTIONS

1. In large, heavy saucepan, heat olive oil. Add onions and garlic.
   Cook on medium heat, stirring frequently, until onions are
   almost translucent, 5 to 6 minutes. Do NOT let either onions
   or the garlic brown.
2. Add carrots, potatoes, and gingerroot to saucepan and cook
   5 minutes to coat well with oil, stirring frequently.
3. Add stock just to cover. Add salt and pepper. Cook over medium
   heat for about 30 minutes, or until vegetables are soft.
4. Purée vegetables and stock in blender or food processor, adding
   more cold stock if necessary.
5. Return purée to saucepan. Stir in the maple syrup. Add more
   stock, as needed, for desired consistency.
6. Adjust seasoning. Heat through and serve.* Add a dollop of sour
   cream or yogurt with chopped parsley or thyme for garnish if
   desired.

*Variation: If you like curry, use only ½ inch of gingerroot and add
½ teaspoon of ground curry. Add it with the vegetables to the saucepan.*

Recipe by Kay Carroll

Roasted Shallot-Maple Vinaigrette

Yield: ⅓ cup

INGREDIENTS
2 tablespoons olive oil
1 small shallot
1 clove garlic
½ teaspoon Dijon-style mustard
1½ tablespoons maple syrup
2 tablespoons sherry (or balsamic vinegar)
1 teaspoon salt
Freshly ground black pepper

DIRECTIONS
1. Preheat the oven to 400°F.
2. In a small baking dish, combine the olive oil, shallot, and garlic.
3. Cover with aluminum foil and roast for 15 minutes or until easily pierced with a fork.
4. Strain the olive oil and set aside, reserving the shallot and garlic. Let cool.
5. In a blender or food processor, combine the reserved shallot, garlic, mustard, maple syrup, sherry or vinegar, and salt. Blend until smooth.
6. With the machine running, gradually add the reserved olive oil in a thin stream.
7. Season with pepper.

This recipe can be used as a salad dressing but also tastes especially delicious drizzled over warm vegetables!

Recipe by Kay Carroll

The Joys of Drudgery

"IT'S A MADNESS," Rob Lamothe says of sugaring. "It possesses you." Laughing heartily and dressed in trademark red suspenders and baseball-style cap, he radiates woodsy, avuncular warmth. Now one of the largest producers in Connecticut with about fifty-six hundred taps, he started in the 1970s making less syrup than I once did. An experimental toolmaker by trade who worked on rocket guidance systems for Hamilton Standard, he's not only a Pied Piper of maple hobbyists leading curious dabblers to tap backyard trees; he's a kind of Johnny Appleseed of small-scale commercial sugaring in northwestern Connecticut and beyond, responsible for the creation or expansion of many operations by selling, installing, and repairing equipment, giving freely of his knowledge, and, most important, infecting customers with boundless enthusiasm for sugaring and life.

Sugaring involves lots of hard work, sometimes downright drudgery. In an age where strenuous physical labor is increasingly avoided, making syrup is paradoxically growing in popularity, perhaps because technology makes it easier than it was years ago. Though its intensity is ameliorated somewhat by the season's brevity, even the ebullient Lamothe gets worn down in January with dawn-to-dusk days of tapping, tubing repairs, and various system upgrades. Once sap begins flowing, his season becomes crazily busy. It's not only from long hours collecting sap and boiling, but due to forty-five hundred visitors coming through the gambrel-roofed sugarhouse sided with yellow clapboards that he and his family built. Despite exhaustingly long hours, Rob entertains people of all ages and stripes as if they were guests, whether individuals, families, or tour groups. The sudden advent of warmer weather and budding trees late in March or early April is a huge letdown, leading to four weeks of tedious cleanup, equipment repairs, and readying the sugarhouse for next season.

However described, maple people feel tied to something larger than themselves, fueling an enthusiasm transcending the normal aversion to backbreaking toil and making the labor its own reward. Exhausting as the work can be, many sugarmakers find it a refreshing refuge from the typical routines of life. Perhaps this is because, like artists, sugarmakers typically have a day job, at least until they hit it big. Sugaring is a passion, a respite from life as usual, a means of self-expression that makes an increasingly abstract world comprehensible. I've heard sugarmakers rhapsodize about connecting to nature, being in touch with earth's cycles, bonding with their great-grandfathers, finding God, or communing with the past. The exact expression of the sentiment doesn't matter. Sugaring seems to evoke a kind of spirituality entwined with and manifest through physical work. Producers may measure the success of a season in gallons of syrup, but it's the process, not the product, that sustains them.

A deeply religious man, Lamothe attends church in Collinsville, just a short walk from my home. When I had a question or problem during my sugaring days, he'd often make a house call after Mass, when his connection to the creator was elevated. On one of those Sunday mornings Lamothe described tapping in the woods on a bitter cold day with a fierce northwest wind. Powdery snow was blowing off the branches as they bent and creaked. Hearing a limb snap, he turned to see penumbral light radiating from behind a tree where it danced and glistened with prismatic colors in the rising sun. All the season's busy effort seemed collapsed in that instant of serenity and peace. Years later, the moment remains vivid, and emotion catches in his throat as he tries to explain. "I know that God had made that moment. It's etched in my heart forever."

• • • • • • •

REVERENCE FOR sugar making often takes a secular twist. From nostalgic perceptions of Native Americans, Currier and Ives prints, notions of laconic Yankees spinning yarns in billows of steam, to today's syrup containers shaped like log cabins, sugaring emanates a

The ever-ebullient Rob Lamothe

romantic mystique. Regardless of today's interconnected realities, the literature and lore of sugaring have shaped the image of an individualistic, off-the-grid, self-sufficient activity where a deep relationship with the land is paramount. "It is that happiest of combinations, a commercial affair which is also an annual rite, even an act of love," wrote Dartmouth College English professor Noel Perrin in his elegiac 1972 book, *Amateur Sugar Maker.*

Perrin, who died in 2004 at age seventy-seven, grew up in and around New York City but in 1963 bought a farm in Thetford Center, Vermont. It served as home and writing muse. Here he built an eighty-eight-square-foot sugarhouse near a dirt road roughly a hundred feet from the Pompanoosuc River "in conscious admiration of Henry David Thoreau." Like his mentor, he vividly records the process of construction and meticulously accounts for costs down to the penny.

Perrin bought a two-by-six Grimm evaporator and made as much as fifty-seven gallons of syrup from 104 taps, some of which he sold to the Globe Corner Bookstore on Boston's Freedom Trail, where his books were also available. Perhaps no one has rendered sugaring in such straightforward yet poetic terms. We share in his worry that a dirt floor may thaw during a boil, causing his evaporator to tilt and burn, and his pleasure in using a hydrometer, an instrument of science that "makes sense to the eye." He relates some sugaring history, rails against weather that produces a "deceitful" season, and delights in chickadees, snow fleas, and other natural phenomena. He describes his rural neighbors with affection and humor, from the town selectman and builder who helped install his evaporator to the man from Corinth who collected sap with two horses and a sled.

Capturing in few words the essence of his world for the sophisticated, urbane readers of the *New Yorker*, where part of the book first appeared, Perrin notes that "gravity and wood are the chief natural resources of a Vermont farm." Reinforcing long-held attitudes among the public and many small-time sugarmakers, he writes: "When you're producing a sacred article, you don't have to maximize your cash return."

A couple generations before Perrin's experiment as a gentleman farmer, Scott and Helen Nearing tapped America's back-to-the-land homesteading vein, stepping out of the mainstream and into a somewhat ascetic life built around sugaring as a self-reliant means to earn a living. Scott was an economist and passionate exponent of country life, labor, peace, and leftist causes. His beliefs cost him a college professorship. Helen was a musician. Both of them strong and preternaturally energetic, they "thumbed their noses at city life" in the heart of the Great Depression and bought a rundown farm "on a side hill of a valley directly facing Stratton Mountain" near Jamaica, Vermont. They did so out of deeply held philosophical yearnings to simplify life, control their livelihood, make contact with nature, and find time for "study, teaching, writing, music and travel." They grew much of their own food and constructed several stone buildings during two decades on the land. Sugaring, as well as lecturing and writing, were their source of cash. They found that even "novices in maple production can turn their energy and ingenuity into a craft that offers scope for imagination and new ideas, and pays sufficient financial returns to provide a simple, but adequate living."

By their example and writings, the Nearings became icons of back-to-the-land homesteading and were influential in the 1960s agrarian commune movement. Published in 1950, *The Maple Sugar Book: Together with Remarks on Pioneering as a Way of Living in the Twentieth Century* probably contains the most comprehensive history of sugaring available, along with instructional advice on making syrup and sugar, a guide to marketing, and recipes. "A life as well as a living" was their passionate call to self-sufficiency and contact with nature. "Anyone who has ever sugared remembers the poesy of it, to the end of his days," the Nearings wrote lyrically. "When the time of year comes round with sap rising and snow melting, there is an insistent urge to take one's part in the process—to tap the trees, to gather the sap, to boil out the sweet syrup of the maple." In such words I find a secular echo of Rob Lamothe's revelation.

. . . .

WHILE THE NEARINGS might be an extreme example, their back-to-the-land gospel resonates with many sugarmakers who hunger for some measure of financial independence entwined with an almost spiritual contact with nature and creation of something tangible and pure. A few years ago I visited Erica Andrews, then at Hurricane Farm in Scotland, Connecticut, a hardscrabble slice of southern New England she cultivated with her husband, Chris. She was dressed in a sweatshirt, work pants, and ski hat beneath which there was a big smile and thick blond braids. Her kids darted around like wood sprites as we talked. Fiercely individualistic, she wanted to live as independently as possible. The farm was named for a hurricane lamp, something the wildest storm can't extinguish.

Growing up in suburbia and earning a British literature degree with a minor in theater and photography, Erica never expected to be a farmer. Her agricultural odyssey started when she and Chris were dating and he decided he wanted a couple of chickens. Soon they had more chickens, a garden, and were raising turkeys. She was waitressing in a martini lounge at the Mohegan Sun casino, and he was teaching school when their daughter was born in January 2004. At that point, they decided to supplement their income by freezing and canning vegetables, which also enabled Erica to be a stay-at-home mom. In spring, she sugared over an open fire with a couple of chafing dishes resting on concrete blocks, making two gallons the first year and three the second. She started baking breads for sale. Hungry for knowledge, she attended livestock auctions and began buying and selling animals, sold food at farmers' markets, and made contacts in the agricultural community.

They had been looking for a house for the better part of two years when they bought Hurricane Farm in 2008, a bargain fixer-upper on just a few acres. She termed the place a natural farm, not organic, but said that they lived an organic lifestyle, meaning close to the land. Though her life has now moved on, farming routines worked well for the family at the time. It allowed her long hours with the children, who saw the fruits of hard work and knew where their food came from, she told me when we sat on a picnic table near her sugarhouse while her then six-year-old played in melting snow, occasionally tasting syrup.

A distinctive structure, the sugarhouse featured a cupola-topped gable roof supported by cedar posts and open on all but one side where it was attached to another farm building. Between posts, firewood was stacked, creating temporary walls. "We're outside people," she said, "and though sleet and rain make it tough sometimes, we want to enjoy outside weather." The small, single-pan, foot-and-a-half-by-three-foot evaporator, purchased on credit around the time they bought the house, yielded twelve gallons of syrup in 2009, its first year. They tapped seventy-five trees on their own and neighboring land using tubing fed into five-gallon pails resting on the ground. In addition to syrup and fruits and vegetables, the farm produced eggs, beef, pork, turkeys, sheep, ducks, and rabbits for pets. They ran a meat-based Community Supported Agriculture program and were vendors at the Coventry Farmers' Market a few towns away, the state's largest.

Rough around the edges and with evidence of many projects in progress, Hurricane Farm was a throwback by a couple of generations to when rural Connecticut was full of small places that grew a variety of crops sustaining families. "Being as self-sufficient as possible is the heart of my ambition," Erica said with religious conviction as she opened the firebox and tossed in a few chunks of wood. "It's what makes me thrive." I never asked if she'd ever heard of the Nearings, but articulate and energetic, she is among their direct spiritual descendants. The way of the future, she postulated, is for people to do more for themselves on their own land, or buy directly from small local farmers. Sugaring teaches patience and the need to slow down and be aware of the world around you, that things come in their moment. "I feel like I'm dancing with nature," she said with a wide smile.

· · · · · · · ·

FOR BRUCE GILLILAN of Fletcher, Vermont, sugaring is not only a connection to the land, but a legacy that has long infused family life with meaning, an unbroken chain stretching back generations. Bruce sugars in a country of tiny towns and modest houses set in rolling green hills patched with forest and fields north and just a bit east of Burlington. It's prime sugaring country where hay is also regularly cut and a few horses or cattle are pastured. J. R. Sloan's Green Mountain Mainlines, the nation's largest sugaring operation, using sap from about 130,000 taps, according to Bruce, is headquartered in town, and the roadside welcome sign greeting travelers depicts an old-time sugarhouse.

The first time I pulled into his driveway at the very beginning of April a few years ago, temperatures were climbing toward eighty and the season was ending early, though the high peaks of the Green Mountains not too far distant were still capped with snow. A square-jawed, plainspoken man with penetrating brown eyes, Bruce is a vice president with Leader Evaporator in Swanton, Vermont, a short ride from the Canadian border. You might think that after forty years at the country's largest maple equipment manufacturer, selling and installing evaporators and troubleshooting sugarhouse problems, he'd have a largely analytical approach to the business. But maple remains deeply personal.

Bruce's grandfather started sugaring in the early 1900s; his father continued the operation, and Bruce grew up in it. Now his son Bradley, the eldest of four, sugars with him and also works for Leader. Knowing the time and effort that go into the frenetic season, the "guys in the shop think I'm crazy," he laughed, shaking his head. "But I can't put a value on the days I spent working beside my dad and the time it gives me with my son." Bruce and his dad would collect sap together. When partway through, his father would fire the evaporator, and Bruce would finish gathering. When Bradley turned ten, the three of them collected together, and Bruce thought his dad would head to the sugarhouse to light the arch when about halfway done. Instead, he sent Bruce to the sugarhouse so he could keep collecting with his grandson. Bruce chokes up as memories flood back. "I didn't get it until later," he said. It's no surprise the operation is called Gillilan Family Maple.

With Bruce at the controls, I rode the draw bar of a blue tractor as we headed through a meadow, crossed a brook, and entered the woods on a rutted path. "It's a bit muddy back there," he warned as we approached a board-and-batten pump house beneath evergreens. "We usually sugar until the tenth or even the fifteenth of the month, but with this weather we're just about done." Crisscrossed with blue and black tubing, the maple orchard is punctuated with pine and hemlock and a smattering of oak. Normally he puts out about eight hundred taps, but this year he only had time to set two-thirds of that amount. "The property has potential for twelve hundred, maybe thirteen hundred," he said with a wave of his hand.

Back in 2010, the sugarhouse was fairly deep in the woods, built of rough vertical boards darkened with age. He told me about an experimental RO—a reverse-osmosis machine—that Bradley built, as we looked over the two-and-a-half-by-ten-foot evaporator sitting on a concrete pad. Bradley is good at tinkering, he said wistfully, something he got from his grandfather. The family's first sugarhouse was built nearby in 1906 but had to be moved downhill a few hundred yards because a downdraft on a stiff south wind would blow flames out of the firebox door. He and Bradley were thinking about a new one close to the road where they could attract visitors and make it easier for families to stop by.

The woods were filled with ghosts and memories. Bruce pointed to tapped trees that were too small when he began working here with his dad, and lines that were strung by Brad. He showed me where he and his son were thinning out the softwoods, but not too quickly, lest the maples get sun-scald from a sudden increase in light. His dad died in these woods, marking a home site for Bradley. He was crushed by a falling tree. Bruce's eyes dampened as he showed me the spot.

Returning from the woods, we entered the canning room attached to a gambrel-roofed garage his father had built in 1985 and also used as a workshop. With its knotty-pine walls and gleaming stainless-steel counter, it seemed like a cross between a cozy cabin and a chemistry lab. The walls were filled with blue, red, and yellow ribbons and plaques the family had earned for its syrup. There's an award to Bruce's dad from the Franklin County Maplerama for lifetime service. Brad was on the committee that made the decision, and got to present his grandfather's award. "Dad built the garage," Bruce said smiling, "and added the canning room later." They used to can in the garage at the house but had to thoroughly clean after each use because "Mom's car had to go back in."

When my wife Mary and I paid Bruce a visit after sugaring season in 2014, he had a bigger tractor, and the roadside sugarhouse had become a reality. He and Bradley had built it into what was once the garage portion of the building where they'd done canning. When we arrived, Bruce was in the process of lining the interior with white-coated metal to provide washable walls. The wood-fired evaporator that Bradley had designed gleamed. Just that morning, Bruce had been testing a new filter press with clear plastic plates that was lighter and less expensive than metal models. It also enabled an operator to observe the syrup as it was processed. Bruce was sure it would catch on among producers.

While we were at the sugarhouse, a few of Bruce's grandchildren stopped by with his wife and daughter-in-law. Among them were Bradley's young sons, Xavier and Gavin, both of whom now drill holes, tap in spouts, and hang buckets on their own trees. Regardless of process innovations or the weather, Bruce Gillilan felt good about the future of sugaring.

◦ ◦ ◦ ◦ ◦ ◦ ◦ ◦

THE FIRST THING you notice when stepping into Lyle Merrifield's sugarhouse in Gorham, Maine, is his collection of antique maple artifacts. Displayed are all manner of spiles and buckets—wooden and metal—syrup jugs, sugar molds, and other tools of the trade, along with quaint images of sugaring. But unlike the objects he so carefully exhibits, the gable-roofed, vertically sided sugarhouse with an ell for a salesroom is fairly new, bright and airy with lots of windows, including a transom over the double doors. A carpenter by trade, Lyle built the place himself, mostly using timber cut and milled on his property.

Golden retriever by his side, the big, gentle man in his thirties, president of the Maine Maple Producers Association, smiled broadly as he joyfully took me through the spacious building immediately behind his home. Enthusiasm rose off him like steam from a raging evaporator. Not from a sugaring family, he had his first taste in kindergarten on a class outing to tap a tree. He remembers it clearly, the bus driver wielding a carpenter's brace and drilling the hole. A few years later he made some syrup with the Scouts, but not until his early twenties did he really get started.

Lyle lives on the twenty-five acres where he grew up in a now suburbanizing area. It's a self-described "gentleman's farm" where he bales hay and raises beef for hamburger, but his passion is maple, even though most of his six to eight hundred taps using vacuum tubing are on neighboring property. He sees advantages to sugaring in thickly settled areas, and tours are a mainstay of his business, with frequent visits by school groups.

Cheerfully entrepreneurial, he gets over four thousand visitors on Maine Maple Sunday weekend and sells, in those two days, over five hundred gallons of syrup, some of which he buys in bulk from other state sugarmakers. Two dozen friends and family members man the farm and serve thousands of maple soft-serve ice cream cups. They go through a hundred pounds of pancake mix, and people wait in line for up to an hour. He sells maple-coated nuts, tubs of maple cream and maple butter, and can't keep up with the demand for candy. His maple cotton candy is popular, and he graciously gave me a container of the woolly stuff for each for my children.

Like other sugarmakers, Lyle thrives on hard work, being outdoors, contact with friends and family, and experiencing seasonal change. You wouldn't think of him as a historian, at least not in the tweedy professorial way, but there's something that fascinates him about maple's uniquely tangible heritage, which is manifested in the artifacts he keeps on walls and shelves. He might not have generations of sugarmakers in his family like Bruce and Bradley Gillilan, but he feels deeply connected to the larger collective kin of sugarmakers.

Perhaps it comes from his time spent handling carpentry tools, but he's fascinated by the progress of technology that speaks to past lives—even something as simple as the transition from homemade wooden taps fashioned from hollowed sumac twigs to metal ones of iron, steel, aluminum, and stainless, and then plastic taps in various colors and formulations for use with tubing. Such objects "have a lot to teach about how and why people did things and the way in which they lived," he told me with reverence in his voice. Not content with mere static displays, he sometimes sets up iron kettles on wooden tripods to demonstrate colonial boiling. He envisions himself on history's continuum, seeing in his syrup not only the weight and density of sugar, but of time. He's never alone, even when he's by himself, he assured me.

· · · · · · ·

LIKE LYLE, Mike Girard has a large collection of sugaring artifacts that he displays at meetings and in his sugarhouse, home, and business office. He feels a similar connection to a collective sugaring heritage that goes beyond a general sense of history. His part in the continuum of maple culture is deeply personal because he has attached himself to a piece of sloping sugarbush that's been tapped for over a century and a quarter, by him since 1976. The land is his touchstone. More than ownership, his relation to the land is one of belonging.

Though discouraged by his grandfather who sugared in Quebec, Mike began his maple ventures in 1960 at age eleven after observing some roadside buckets on a trip with his dad. Soon he was tapping on the family dairy farm in Simsbury, Connecticut, using an evaporator his father bought. Eventually the operation grew to six hundred taps. He is an athletic and articulate man with neatly trimmed dark hair who runs a construction company displaying a bulldozer on its logo. You wouldn't immediately peg him as someone deeply in love with trees and a plot of land for its natural, sustainable values, but sugaring has made it so.

Mike recalls making maple candy instead of doing homework, selling it at recess during fourth and fifth grades, much to the chagrin of his Catholic school nuns. Eventually he built a sugarhouse on the farm, but wanted more than roadside trees. After diligent searching, he bought land and a sugarhouse just about a mile south of Vermont on Number Nine Road in Heath, Massachusetts, a town of about four hundred souls. Although it's eighty-five miles from his Simsbury home, a trip that gets longer as he gets older, he fell in love with the property and its history of maple production.

The operation was begun by George Brown in 1887, and Mike speaks about it as one might an inheritance. He considers himself a steward, another in a line of several sugarmakers who have tried their luck here with nature and a bit of tinkering talent. Though it has been more than a century since Brown's horses collected sap, and throughout the years Mike has installed over three and a half miles of vacuum tubing through the woods, he feels a bond with this land and its past that almost makes the differences in technology illusory. The sugarhouse has been rebuilt a couple of times and expanded, but the structure would probably be familiar to Brown despite an oil-fired evaporator and installation of battens over gaps between the old boards so wide "you could throw your hat through." For decades the woods have been carefully managed for maples, and though storms have wrought sudden and sometimes violent modifications, the place has a purposeful, time-defiant personality formed by years of sugaring. "I suppose there will always need to be changes to keep maple viable," Mike observed, "but it's the memories that keep sugaring and the place alive."

Some memories are bittersweet, such as the closure a couple of years ago of Peters General Store about three hundred yards down the road. For almost a century, they had sold syrup from Mike's sugarhouse. Other memories bring a smile, such as the two dozen times he won first prize at the Heath Fair, and the other ribbons he's garnered.

Mike took me through the cupola-topped board-and-batten sugarhouse with its adjacent two-bay woodshed. It holds thirty-three cords no longer needed since the purchase in 2000 of an oil-fired three-and-a-half-by-twelve-foot Darveau "Mystique" evaporator with digital auto draw-off, preheater, and air injection. He describes the machine as looking like "a locomotive that runs nowhere." The sugaring operation is like a living thing to Mike, and as we stand in the sugarhouse he recalls his predecessors, the evaporators they used, the number of taps they had, and the price they were paid for a gallon of syrup. He knows when the roof was rebuilt and the sugarhouse moved eight feet back from the road. These stories are his patrimony, his sustenance.

Mike remembers every ice storm, tornado, and gypsy moth outbreak that damaged his trees. He knows when each part of the sugarbush was thinned, and has planted plots of experimental "supersweet" trees from Cornell and the University of Vermont. He started with one thousand taps and went to thirty-five hundred by using trees all over town in partnership with the grandson of Francis Galipo, the man who succeeded Brown in 1929. He worked with the young man from the time the kid was twelve until his untimely death in a snowmobile accident at thirty-two.

Now down to about eight hundred taps, Mike's son Mikey, who has assisted him for over thirty years, does most of the boiling and sugarbush work, with Mike as his assistant. Mikey is strong and rangy, sharing his father's delight in a sugarmaker's life. He says sugaring frees one's mind to "think about life and where you're going."

Mike Girard may have handed much of the operation over to his son, but he remains embedded in this landscape as much as his predecessors. His presence will be felt as long as there are maple trees here and people to care for them.

Orange Maple Glazed Chicken

Yield: 20 Chicken Wings

INGREDIENTS

1½ cups buttermilk
⅓ cup maple syrup
2 oranges, seeded, peeled, and sectioned
1 teaspoon ground cinnamon
20 chicken wings

DIRECTIONS

1. Mix all ingredients except chicken wings in a blender to make a coarse puree.
2. Put wings and puree in a gallon-size plastic bag and refrigerate for at least 2 hours, turning occasionally.
3. Grill wings, periodically basting with the marinade, until they are cooked through, being careful to avoid scorching.

Recipe by Karen Broderick

Maple Parsnips

Yield: variable

INGREDIENTS
Parsnips
Maple syrup

DIRECTIONS
1. Scrub the parsnips until clean.
2. Cut parsnips into pieces. (Homegrown parsnips need not be cored, but store-bought ones tend to have a woody center that may need to be removed.)
3. Steam cubed parsnips until tender, about 10 minutes.
4. Mash and add maple syrup to taste.

This recipe tastes best when you use dark maple syrup! Its more assertive flavor perfectly balances the flavor of the parsnips.

Recipe by Pat Dubos

The End of Maple?

KILLERS ARE ON THE LOOSE. Invading aliens are attacking the old industrial city of Worcester, Massachusetts, and surrounding towns. Almost thirty-four thousand street and yard trees in 110 square miles, largely maples, have disappeared. An additional fourteen hundred acres of forested land have been stripped of maples, birches, and elms. Entire residential neighborhoods are practically denuded, leaving barren streets and unshaded homes. The invaders have coal-black bodies stippled with white spots, six bluish feet, and striped antennae that can be more than twice their body length. Fearsome-looking creatures, they are fortunately no more than an inch and a quarter long.

It sounds like a science fiction plot from some Hollywood B movie requiring a superhero's intervention. But there's no unspeakable horror threatening from outer space, and the courageous champion fighting this calamity is neither more powerful than a locomotive nor leaps tall buildings at a single bound. He's a soft-spoken entomologist with a beard and ponytail who wears jeans and work boots.

If you think the mundane terrestrial origins of this animal or its diminutive size is reason not to fear the end of maple trees in our region, then you probably are not aware that the American chestnut was once a dominant forest tree throughout most of New England, used for everything from fence rails to pianos and utility poles, until a blight caused by nearly invisible fungal spores imported from Asia wiped out almost all of them in little more than a generation. Persistent stump sprouters, these woodland giants are now just an occasional large shrub. Look at some old postcards and marvel at the colonnades of grand elms that once graced the avenues of almost every town and city in the Northeast and Midwest until Dutch elm disease made quick work of them, leaving once-leafy neighborhoods as barren as the residential streets in the Greendale and Burncoat neighborhoods of Worcester are today.

So far, the Asian long-horned beetle (*Anoplophora glabripennis*), or ALB, as it is popularly known, has remained a scourge of urban areas because, as crossroads of international commerce, they are likely to receive nonnative invasive species as unwanted hitchhikers on pallets and in shipping containers delivered to the businesses clustered there. No commercial sugarbush has yet been affected, but ALB has been a hot topic at maple meetings and around evaporators for several years. If "established here, it could be one of the most destructive and costly invasive species ever to enter the United States," according to the U.S. Department of Agriculture. The insect is capable of riddling a tree with three-eighths-inch borings, about a taphole's diameter, and not only compromise its vascular system, but weaken its structural integrity so severely that the trees fall apart and simply collapse. Uncontrolled, ALB could quickly spread to sugar orchards and put an end to syrup production. ALB kills trees. It could kill an entire food industry.

With piercing blue eyes, a marquee-quality name, and a fierce determination to fulfill a mission, Clint McFarland is one of the Worcester area's leading antagonists of ALB. He works for USDA's Animal and Plant Health Inspection Service—better known by its acronym APHIS—as project director of ALB eradication. On a snow-frosted January day we met at his office, a sprawling single-story structure on the outskirts of downtown. He escorted me to a small room among a warren of crowded cubicles. The tight space was busy with cabinets, a couple of desks, computer terminals, and teetering piles of paper. A soft-voiced man of energetic enthusiasm preaching a gospel of awareness, he was eager for me to meet the beetles, because a heads-up public was the best weapon against spread of the scourge.

Often citizens are the first to find new infestations, like the woman who discovered the insects in her yard and worried that they might bite or sting her grandchildren. Tracking down an image of ALB with a few keystrokes on her computer, she discovered that government authorities were interested in sightings. Within twelve hours, a SWAT team of bug hunters was in her yard taking down the trees.

Keen to have me know his nemesis in all its manifestations, McFarland gathered illustrations, vials, bags, mounted specimens, chunks of wood, and other show-and-tell objects from around the room, explaining each in exact detail, like an athlete or hunter showing off his trophies. Onto the table in front of me he tossed a thick branch perforated with the telltale exit holes of newly emerged adults and the roundish pockmarks carved into the bark where females had chewed nest spots to lay eggs. He had a round latitudinal slice of tree trunk, called a cookie, with a network of cavities and tunnels burrowed by the insects. He showed me the white, pill-shaped eggs, the wormlike off-white larva and pupa, and the glossy-black, white-stippled adults with their widespread antennae. Perfectly still and entombed in a jar, the beetle appeared elegant in its symmetry and simple coloring, though a living one crawling around would have given me the creeps.

McFarland plopped a couple of containers onto the table. Inside appeared to be sawdust. "Frass," he said—a mixture of gnawed wood and bug poop that developing larvae push onto the ground or nearby limbs as they burrow inside a tree. It's one of the telltale signs of ALB, produced during the larval stage when the insects gnaw deep into heartwood to feed on nutrients and carve their network of tunnels. I thought frass might be McFarland's ultimate piece of ALB evidence, but he carefully placed a two-foot-tall log in front of me. It had been cut in quarters the long way and then hinged so that it opened to display interior ALB carvings, intricate lacunae of oval and linear excavations that left the branch a hollowed shell.

Soon we were in a small, dark car with government plates, prowling a predominately single-family middle-class neighborhood barren of trees except for a few spindly saplings at roadside. It had the stark vibe of a fresh subdivision carved into cropland, though the houses had been occupied for at least a couple of generations. McFarland sighed as he showed me photographs taken before the infestation. It had been a handsome street of overarching, mature shade trees. As in much of Worcester, red and Norway maples were common, and once infested they had to come down. They had been replaced by ALB-resistant oaks and other seedlings, but it would be years before those trees cast substantial shadows on the pavement and homes. These new plantings were among tens of thousands being established, including spruce and other evergreens, dogwood and crab apple — signs of perseverance and hope that ALB eradication efforts will not leave these areas naked. Still, the neighborhoods will never look the same without their colorful fall maples, showy spring horse-chestnut flowers, and white birch trunks.

A native of Asia, ALB landed in this country hidden in pallets and shipping crates from the Far East. No one knows when it arrived, but it was first discovered in 1996 in the Greenpoint area of Brooklyn, New York. Since then, it has been found in other nearby areas of New York, the northern New Jersey suburbs, and in and around Chicago. Although ALB was officially declared eradicated in Chicago and parts of New Jersey by 2008 (the same year the Worcester beetles were discovered), a new infestation was found in 2011 in southern Ohio not far from Cincinnati. An infestation in Boston and Brookline that covered ten square miles was declared eradicated in 2014. In addition to maples, ALB attacks elms, willows, birches, ash, and horse chestnut, some of our most commonly planted and beautiful trees found in yards and along streets, as well as in the woods. In all, there are thirteen genera victimized by ALB.

Our next stop was a subdivision that looked like it was built toward the end of the last century. There weren't many large trees in front of the houses, but the yards backed up to scraggly woods where kids played and leaves were tossed in fall. Dozens of these trees, ranging from pole timber to about eighteen inches in diameter, had a string of orange surveyor's tape wrapped around them, mark of a death sentence. McFarland handed me his field glasses, and with his guidance it became easy to see trunks and branches riddled with adult exit holes and the oval bark pits, like scars, where the females had nested. I spotted uneven lumps of frass in the crotch of several branches, as if someone had been sawing into the limbs above.

With binoculars usually around his neck, McFarland might be mistaken for a bird watcher as he lifts them to peer into branches high overhead. He's a lookout. Like a military scout, he's always on watch, ready to detect the slightest sign of the enemy. It's a big job,

Trees infested with Asian long-horned beetle marked for cutting

with millions of trees to keep an eye on, which is why he needs his posse of public eyeballs. In addition to the signs I could see through the lenses or actual sightings of adult insects, he looks for unseasonable leaf yellowing, broken or dying branches, and sap flows caused by excavation wounds.

The beetles are active in summer and early autumn, when a mated female might chew between thirty-five and ninety depressions in the bark, in each one laying an egg that hatches in about ten days to two weeks. The emerging caterpillar burrows through the bark and into the layer of the tree where sap flows, then into the woody tissue to develop and overwinter. In spring, the beetle larvae build a hard case and develop into adults, chewing their way out in summer and leaving those perfectly round exit holes, often with frass beneath them. Adults feed on small twigs and leaves, mate, and die with the advent of cold weather.

McFarland pulled into a vast open area fenced with chain link topped by barbed wire in an industrial section of town. A large yellow sign at the entrance warned the public away from the Asian Long-horned Beetle Disposal/Processing Center. Within a space bounded by a street and old brick industrial buildings were Everests of wood chips steaming with composting warmth in the cold air. Large mobile grinders on dozer tracks with giraffe-neck-like conveyors spewed chipped material with a loud roar. Excavators and bulldozers roamed the property like ersatz mechanical dinosaurs. This was the maple graveyard. Beautiful trees that took decades to reach maturity were cut in their prime and reduced to piles of chips. It was a triumph to detect the pest, cut and transport the trees, but it was sad.

When ALB hits an area, the first step is a quarantine of firewood and other woody material. Fortunately, the beetles don't go very far by themselves. They usual bum a ride in cordwood, logs, and brush. But detection of the beetles is a death sentence for the host tree and those growing nearby. Luckily, chipping to less than an inch also kills the insect. Even if they survive the chopping and grinding, their life cycle is interrupted by lack of moisture and nutrients in the chipped wood, and they go from hazard to harmless under the sharp edge of knife-like blades. The chips can be used as mulch, fuel, or for any other purpose. McFarland smiled and talked over the roar of the grinder while gesturing at the piles. He's optimistic. With vigilance by the public and quick, SWAT team–like responses to destroy infected trees, he thinks ALB can be eradicated in Worcester before it spreads and devastates nearby woodlands, including sugarbushes. Without acute observation and instant response, however, the future of maples would be grim.

Since 2008 over four million host trees have been surveyed, and the effort to determine the outer boundary of the infestation should be complete by autumn 2014. There are eighty state and federal employees engaged in surveying and an additional two hundred contractors. Most work from the ground, but thirty climb trees with rope and harness. About a thousand funnel traps, baited with plant volatiles and pheromones, have been set to capture any nearby beetles. Fortunately, new discoveries and the density of infestation have been declining precipitously—by about 90 percent from 2008 to 2014. McFarland is hopeful that in seven to ten years the area will be declared ALB free. In the meantime, he and others keep a careful watch, check and recheck.

Our last stop was a venerable roadside sugar maple, a big tree with a classic spreading crown, the kind old-time sappers might have put four taps into. At about breast height was a small, bright-red metal tag. "Do Not Tap," it warned. "Treated with IMIDACLOPRID 2010." Sometimes unaffected trees within a quarantine area are treated with this insecticide for at least three years. Injected into the soil or the tree, it spreads throughout the maple's vascular system and kills ALB adults and larvae upon ingestion. It's sometimes used to protect arboreal landmarks. "How long will it take before the sap can be used for syrup?" I asked. McFarland just shrugged. "Not," he said.

* * * * * * * *

ALB IS NOT the first serious threat to maple trees. Over the years there have been pear thrips, tent caterpillars, gypsy moths, and invasive plants like garlic mustard or even an overabundance of deer that inhibit seedling growth. But no threat is possibly as devastating as climate change. Its invisibility, gradual onset, widespread consequences, and political controversy make it particularly pernicious. Regardless that some people don't believe in it, it has already wrought change in the maple industry and may actually benefit some producers, at least for a generation or so.

Octogenarian Alvin Clark points to a large poster-board chart on the wall of his sugarhouse in Langdon, New Hampshire. "I call it seasons of change," he said in a voice as dry as maple bark, "because sugaring starts earlier and ends later." With days of the month from late February to mid-April on the left margin and years across the top, black and red ink shows how much syrup was made on a given day since 1959. Blank spaces with downward arrows drawn through them predominate at the top of the chart in the earlier years, illustrating later starting dates, while similar spaces with an arrow dominate the bottom of the chart in more recent seasons because they end sooner.

The retired loading-dock worker, carpenter, and part-time farmer is a third-generation sugarmaker, and his burly, bearded son David now runs the operation. A sepia-toned photo of Alvin shows a boy in a heavy coat sitting on a log beside a steaming outdoor evaporator in 1939. The wiry old man sighs and for a moment seems to fade into his memory. "Weather patterns have definitely changed," he said softly. "We used to go into the second week of April. Now it ends early in the first week or even at the close of March."

There's a wistful sadness in Clark's assessment, but he won't let it steal his joy. On this late-March day, the board-and-batten sugarhouse in a steep ravine close to the road and near a small stream is full of sweet steam and cheerful visitors, from babes in arms to an elegant gray-haired woman named Tish who's been coming since the 1950s. There's a party atmosphere, with people gathered around the evaporator or seated at a row of bright Formica booths eating chili dogs, doughnuts, Alvin's maple-pecan pie, or bison burgers from David's herd. Some are admiring the old sugar molds, antique buckets, spiles, containers, and pieces of tubing hanging on the walls and suspended from the ceiling. Others are picking at the sugar-on-snow set out in trays, the taffy-like confection so thick and sticky that several of the plastic spoons used for scooping it lay broken nearby. Regardless of how early it comes, we like to celebrate spring with sugaring.

• • • • • • •

WITH SUGARMAKERS notoriously dependent upon and sensitive to the weather, there is hardly a year when conditions seem just right. "Syrup-Makers Not Sweet on High Temps," a headline in the *New Haven Register* read a few years back. "Snow Makes It Harder to Reach Trees, Cold Delays Sap Flow," the *Hartford Courant* reported a couple of years later.

Even the slightest variation in sunlight or temperature due to topography makes a difference. "I seem to be at the wrong elevation this year," Shelburne, Massachusetts, sugarmaker Jim Graves told me when I visited his place at a bend in a dirt road.

Variable weather can present some interesting dilemmas. Though New Portland, Maine, is in an area famous for long months of skiing, there wasn't much snow in Al Bolduc's sugar woods when I visited there a few seasons ago at the end of March. Not only did the trees pop buds early, but Al, a squat man in his seventies at the time, had trouble reaching his taps because they were drilled high in expectation of the usual thick winter blanket.

All agricultural crops are at the mercy of weather, but none is so subject to micro-variations as sugaring. Sugarmakers are canaries in the coal mine when it comes to global climate change, and increasingly they acknowledge the contribution of human activity to a warming world. But while technical advice from scientists and equipment manufacturers on how to deal with warmer seasons is now a common seminar topic at maple meetings, there remain holdouts who deny the impact of humans on climate. Somewhat like Mr. Jones in Bob Dylan's "Ballad of a Thin Man," they know something is happening even if they say they don't know what it is.

Leading scientists in the field of sugaring and maple ecology not only know something is happening, they *do* know what it is. The climate is warming. "Filtering and boiling a sugar solution that has been warmed for hours in a leafless forest, at temperatures that cause microorganisms to grow exponentially, is quite challenging," Tim Wilmot, a maple specialist with the University of Vermont Extension, has written in *Farming: The Journal of Northeast Agriculture.* "Equally challenging is collecting enough sap to make a decent crop of sugar before the maple buds start to swell and ruin the flavor."

• • • • • • • •

ON AN UNUSUALLY warm day at the very beginning of May 2013, I visited Wilmot's colleague, Dr. Timothy Perkins, director of the university's Proctor Maple Research Center, one of the nation's most prestigious institutions of basic and applied research into maple tree health and syrup production. Not far from Burlington, the Proctor Center is on the lower slopes of Mount Mansfield just outside the tiny village of Underhill Center, a cluster of older houses with a gas station, country store, church, and white clapboard town hall, all emblematic of bucolic, rural Vermont. Heading west out of town, I took a rising dirt road through a forest of mostly maple and birch. Blue and green tubing strung through the woods glowed in the sun, and nodding yellow trout lily and spring beauty were blooming on the forest floor. In less than a mile, I arrived at a clutch of buildings built on uneven ground at the edge of the forest. Among them was a large board-and-batten sugarhouse with classic cupola, a barn-like production research facility filled with gleaming stainless-steel evaporators and tanks, the squat block-and-shingle laboratory and office with a standing seam roof, and a tiny red shed that is the original 1947 lab.

The maple sugaring season "has shifted significantly over the past several decades throughout the northeast." It "begins approximately 8.2 days earlier in the calendar year than it did 40 years ago" and ends "approximately 11.4 days earlier . . . representing a loss of approximately 10% of the total season," the athletic, soft-spoken Perkins testified before Congress in 2007. Acknowledging that technical advances in sap collection like tubing and vacuum extraction "may help to offset yield losses resulting from a reduction in season duration . . . a loss of the maple industry in the U.S. within the next 100 years would appear to be inevitable" as the freeze-and-thaw cycle "conditions for sapflow, become less prevalent."

Perkins's prediction of loss was for the commercial maple industry. He thought it likely there would continue to be hobby producers, but that commercial production would become less and less economically viable. Furthermore, Perkins testified that "in the long term (100-plus years), climate change is expected to shift forest composition, resulting in a loss of the maple-beech-birch as a dominant forest type throughout much of New England and New York."

With the sugaring season over, the wiry Perkins seemed relaxed. Instead of jacket and tie like he'd worn before Congress, he had on a loose-fitting shirt and shorts. A couple of days of stubble bristled on his cheeks as we sat in his small, comfortably crowded office with a metal desk, couch, and small wooden table piled with papers. His diplomas and a galaxy of sticky notes were on the wall. Family photos sat on the windowsill. The sugaring season wasn't totally over at Proctor, he said, since a colleague was experimenting with birch, a tree with a later sap run. A hint of smile stole over his face. "We've thought of combining them," he said, "a birch and maple syrup mixture. We might call it birple." I groaned. "That's why I'm not the marketing guy," he laughed.

His demeanor changed quickly as he told me that the data on which his congressional testimony was based have been updated through 2012, and while "numbers have shifted a little," the trends remain the same, the conclusions largely correct. When we last talked in

September 2014, he was reanalyzing the data to incorporate the most recent season.

Despite the long-term prognosis for the maple industry, Perkins was engaged. There was energy in his voice, a rhythm of enthusiasm for his work. New questions come up, he said, because thousands of sugarmakers with plenty of time on their hands while sap boils keep making observations and test speculations. The "aha" moments multiply in intriguing and unexpected ways.

In the northern reaches of the maple zone, global warming may even have a temporary beneficial effect on sugaring, Perkins speculated. He leaned back in his chair, smiling as surprise stole across my face. Autumn has its own freeze-thaw oscillation, and while the sugar content of sap is lower, trees could be successfully tapped. Traditional tapping will continue to come early. With autumn coming later and spring arriving earlier, it's possible to have the two sugaring opportunities meet and have one season that extends from perhaps the middle of November to the end of February. He's begun thinking about research into the consequences and opportunities of a fall season.

As Perkins indicated, climate change is a two-pronged threat to the sugaring world. The most immediate concern is sufficient temperature fluctuation to induce sap flow. But the long-term fate of maple trees themselves is also at stake and will affect not just the syrup business, but the ecology of the region and the multibillion-dollar tourist industry that depends on sugar maples for flaming orange and some of the brightest reds in the Northeast's palette of fall color.

· · · · · · · ·

SUGAR MAPLES are Dr. Charles Canham's favorite tree, and he has spent much of his career dedicated to studying their ecology and health, probably publishing more papers on the topic than anyone else. A scientist at the nonprofit Cary Institute of Ecosystem Studies in Millbrook, New York, since 1984, he has a rich voice inspiring confidence, and speaks with a compelling professorial logic. Even under the worst climate-change scenarios, the disappearance of sugar maples is unlikely over the next century, he told me, though they may become less common, and seedling survival and abundance may be reduced by deer overbrowsing and by warmth-induced new pests and pathogens.

While in fifty to eighty years the climate in Hartford, Connecticut, may be like that in present-day Richmond, Virginia, adult forest trees are extremely resilient. In fact, because temperate forests occur over the widest range of conditions, they will lag behind many other indicators of climate change, Canham said. Though the climate is warming, he's confident that sugar maples will long continue as part of the New England forest. After all, there are some sugar maples in Louisiana. But the fluctuating temperature conditions to produce sap runs may decline and then disappear from southern New England over the next several generations. He sees ALB as a much greater and immediate threat to maples, one that could make the species go the way of the American chestnut if APHIS isn't successful. As for climate change, "maples aren't butterflies."

• • • • • • • •

EVEN IF MAPLES are here to stay, at least for a few generations, the question of temperature oscillation leading to sap flows will remain a conundrum, because climate change is not a straight-line trend on a graph. With its crazy yearly variations, weather gets in the way. And regardless of long-term increases in temperature, one of a sugarmaker's biggest concerns is predictability in these times when reliable winter and spring temperatures in many years seem to have been replaced with bedevilingly wild and chaotic fluctuations. It's increasingly hard to know when to tap or make an educated guess on when the season is likely to end. "There are a lot of small sugarmakers in the area who don't bother tapping anymore because the weather is getting too weird," says naturalist Jay Kaplan, for decades doing sugaring demonstrations as director of the Roaring Brook Nature Center in Canton, Connecticut.

Forester Jody Bronson pulls several thick folders out of a battered metal filing cabinet in his office within the repair shop at Great Mountain Forest (GMF), over six thousand privately owned acres in Norfolk and Canaan, Connecticut, forever dedicated to forest management under a federal easement. More at home in the woods than indoors, Bronson is a bearded bear of a man, typically wearing a checked wool shirt and heavy boots. He pulls out the slightly yellowed and dog-eared papers and plops them on his desk, where the computer, documents, pencils, and other office items share space with a few drill bits, machine parts, a pair of vise-grips, and some wire. Besides managing the forest for timber and other products, Bronson runs Coolwater Sugarhouse.

Sugaring began at GMF in 1940 with three hundred taps, a three-by-eight-foot evaporator, and a couple of draft horses named Chubb No. 1 and Chubb No. 2. Now occupying the fourth sugarhouse on the property, the operation has gone from being a profit-making entity to a nonprofit educational organization. Though there are many sugaring operations with a long and proud heritage, Coolwater has something that few others have: records that extend back over sixty years.

The Coolwater documents contain not only the volume of sap collected on various days and the amount of syrup produced; they include the high and low temperature and descriptive information such as cloud cover and wind strength and direction. Phenological information such as sightings of the first robin or bluebird and species of trees budding are noted. Particular sugar maples were carefully measured each year, season after season, for volume of sap and sugar content. Furthermore, the property has a National Weather Service Cooperative Weather Observer Station known as Norfolk 2 sw. At this site, temperature, precipitation, and wind speed and direction are recorded. Readings are also taken to measure evaporation, information valuable in forestry and agriculture. In 1964, the station became one of the first seven Reference Climatological Stations in the country. Readings go back to 1932 when the late Edward "Ted" Childs began recording weather data as part of his master's thesis at Yale's forestry school.

In 1909, Ted Childs's father, Starling W. Childs, and his partner U.S. senator Frederick C. Walcott purchased the first piece of what was to become Great Mountain Forest in pursuit of wildlife and forest management goals. Most of the parcels had been owned by iron companies and repeatedly cut for charcoal to smelt ore, with hemlock groves felled for tanbark used in leather tanning. Where today the rugged slopes are thick with tall mixed hardwoods and islands of pine and hemlock, there were burned-over scrub and brushlands at the turn of the twentieth century.

Heir to his father's property, Ted Childs purchased Walcott's interest and bought more of this heavily glaciated upland underlain by crystalline rock. He created softwood plantations that included exotic conifers, established scientifically monitored plots, protected a few remnant groves of trees over 350 years old, managed habitat to foster wildlife, and promoted education through establishment of the Yale Forestry Camp for student field training. Today the Great Mountain Forest Corporation is in the nature of a charitable land trust overseen by the Childs family and a board of scientific advisers, including Charlie Canham.

With his rough, callused hands, Bronson leafed through the stack of papers on his desk and spread them out for me. There were graphs and photos, handwritten diary-like entries, old-fashioned typescript summaries of past years, and modern spreadsheets comparing data from as early as 1950. The records are meticulous, showing not only gallons of syrup and sap, but dates the buckets were hung, the length of the season, number of trees tapped and number of taps, including the average number of taps per tree. Among the data are the numbers and dates of collections, the sap-to-syrup ratio, and the gross return per tree in quarts and dollars. Operational statistics list cords of wood and the gallons made per cord; total man and truck hours; and collecting, boiling, and tapping times. Bronson also possesses reams of weather data and has summaries of warmest and coolest years, wettest and driest, and inches of snowfall.

A thoughtful man, Bronson feels a delightful weight in this multigenerational legacy entrusted to him, and he treats each sheet of paper as if he were sorting through a box in a rare-book library. He started citing statistics, almost chanting, in awe of what he was holding and reading. He looked up at me and grinned. "I just love this stuff," he said. "There may be two feet of snow on the ground, but sugaring means spring. Soon the woods will be alive with insects and critters."

Though they're down to 130 buckets and about 300 taps on gravity tubing in an operation that once boasted thousands of taps, Bronson's passion has only grown since the new sugarhouse opened in 2012.

Built of lumber harvested off the property and containing a shiny
new evaporator under a green standing-seam roof, it exists primarily
for public education. Where once the Coolwater Sugarhouse was in
the vanguard of new technology with an aluminum tubing system
in the 1940s and the first reverse osmosis machine in Connecticut
during the early 1970s, its mission today is stirring interest among
the young for syrup and forestry. A natural teacher who radiates excitement, Bronson entertains Scout, church, and school groups. He
welcomes families and anyone else who wants to spend time enjoying
the lore and magic of sugaring. He likes showing kids around the
evaporator and having them help collect sap. "Damn, it's fun," he said.

Paul K. Barten, the executive director of GMF between 2009 and
2014 and a professor of forest resources at the University of Massachusetts, shares Bronson's fervor. "A traditional wood-fired operation
is an opportunity to tell a story that touches not only on sustainable
forestry, but community, history, and wildlife management," he told
me on a 2012 visit to the nineteenth-century farmhouse that serves as
GMF headquarters. "Something as simple as thinning a sugar orchard
to promote tree growth has so many implications. It's equally about
cuttings to fire the evaporator, opening the woods for wildlife, and
what's on the breakfast table. It's a means to get folks interested and
involved in the forest."

With his own training and expertise in hydrology and climatology
and GMF's wealth of weather and sugaring records, Barten seemed
to have found an ideal place for drawing conclusions about climate
change. A lanky man with a neat salt-and-pepper beard, Barten
leaned back in his chair, pulled off his glasses, and sighed. The data is
"messy and complex," he told me. "And tangling with two voluminous
data sets is like trying to take a sip from a fire hose. The records are
so meticulous that they may capture too much natural variability.
Lots of number-crunching grunt work has to precede analysis before
conclusions emerge."

Barten listed some of the variables that are hard to fathom: the
previous year's growing season, snowpack, forest maturity, soil moisture, and sunlight. He was determined to wrestle with the data Bronson holds so dearly, but acknowledged that it will be neither easy nor
quick. While observing that anecdotally the season is starting earlier

and ending earlier, with fewer sap-flow days that should be an omen for sugarmakers, he thinks that sugaring, with its wide-ranging variables subject to frustratingly wild vacillations in weather, might not be the best poster child for measuring climate change.

Back at the shop, Bronson waxed poetic over the deep connection to a place that sugaring inspires. He laughed as he told me of the time he took a school group into the sugarhouse on a quiet day when he wasn't boiling, flipped on the lights, and found a red squirrel floating in the evaporator. He quickly had someone distract the children and grabbed the creature. "Did you wring him out before you tossed him?" I asked. He chuckled and gave me a big smile.

As much as he loves sugaring and despite the new sugarhouse, Bronson shook his head sadly and told me it's not a good time to invest in southern New England maple. "The weather is on a rollercoaster of crazy extremes," he said, "and the trees don't know what to do." Of course, if sugaring ends it won't happen quickly. It will be a slow decline. But for a forester trained to measure time in decades of tree growth, it seemed more imminent than it might to the average person.

Regardless of what happens in southern New England, as Dr. Perkins of the University of Vermont pointed out, the northern regions of the maple world might experience a generational boom from a warming climate. With the percentage expansion of taps in double digits over the past few years, mostly close to either side of the Canadian border, the decline in sugaring to the south and its significance may be little noticed at first. In fact, over 90 percent of syrup is produced in areas that will benefit, at least temporarily, from a warming climate. Of course, if sugaring comes to an end south of Vermont, there will be much greater cultural and environmental disruptions than changes in maple sap flow.

Even if Bronson's worst fears are realized, Coolwater may be among the last sugarhouses in Connecticut. Freezing winters with deep snow have long given Norfolk the reputation as the state's "icebox." If sugaring is going to happen anywhere in the Constitution State, it will be here with the likes of Jody Bronson breathing in the steam and throwing wood in the firebox.

Maple Marinated Kielbasa

Yield: variable

INGREDIENTS
Kielbasa sausage
Maple syrup

DIRECTIONS
1. Slice the kielbasa lengthwise, then cut into 3-inch pieces.
2. Marinate the slices overnight in maple syrup.
3. Cook the marinated kielbasa on a grill until done.

The maple syrup is the perfect counterpoint to the garlicky kielbasa. A slight maple flavor infuses the sausages, and the grilling caramelizes the syrup, resulting in a delicious crust!

Recipe by Trevor Soulé

Maple-Marinated Roasted Salmon

Yield: 6 servings

INGREDIENTS

¾ cup maple syrup
2 tablespoons peeled and grated fresh gingerroot
2 tablespoons fresh lemon juice
2 tablespoons reduced-sodium soy sauce
½ teaspoon ground black pepper
¼ teaspoon salt
One 2¼-pound salmon fillet (skin on)

DIRECTIONS

1. Preheat oven to 400°F.
2. In a large baking dish, combine maple syrup, gingerroot, lemon juice, soy sauce, pepper, and salt.
3. Place salmon, skin side up, in dish. Cover, refrigerate, and marinate 15 minutes. Turn, marinate an additional 15 minutes.
4. Line a large baking pan with parchment paper. Place salmon on parchment paper, skin side down. Brush with marinade and place in the oven. Roast salmon 10 minutes. Brush fish with remaining marinade and continue roasting until flesh flakes when tested with a fork (about 10 to 15 minutes more).

If you don't have any fresh lemons, you can use fresh lime juice or white wine vinegar as a substitute for the fresh lemon juice.

Recipe by Nancy Reynolds

Hot Rocks and
Bubbling Cauldrons

DRESSED IN BUCKSKINS sewn from the hide of a deer he killed with a flint-tipped arrow, James Dina leaned over a small fire he started with friction sticks. Flames were licking at several rocks about the size of large potatoes. With twin sticks formed into tongs, he lifted five of the rocks, one at a time, and placed them in a sap-filled wooden trough he had hollowed out of a log by burning and scraping. After just a couple of hot stones, the gallon and a half of liquid began to sizzle, froth, and foam as sweet steam wafted into frigid air. Although it was too cold for sap to drip, he showed a clutch of people gathered to watch his sugaring demonstration at the Institute for American Indian Studies in Washington, Connecticut, where he had gashed a maple with a homemade stone axe. From the wound, he had run a long sumac stick with the pith hollowed out to a birch-bark sap-collection vessel situated at the base of the tree.

Dina is lithe and muscular for a man in his seventies, with long gray hair pulled back in a ponytail. Though his heritage is not Native American, he's not just some fair-weather weekend reenactor. His knowledge runs deep and well beyond the many books he's read or demonstrations he's witnessed. A self-styled "primitive technologist," he experiments creating pre-Columbian objects using the same tools and materials that were available to native people.

Dina has enjoyed "playing Indian" since he was a kid. In 1985, while he was in his early forties, inspiration struck this MIT-educated mechanical engineer and classical guitarist, and he built a birch-bark canoe with stone age tools. He paddled the vessel from his hometown of Windsor, Connecticut, almost to the Canadian border with only equipment and supplies such as indigenous people would carry. Afterward, he wrote *Voyage of the Ant,* a time-bending book of perseverance, survival, and ingenuity.

While never again embarking on a project so ambitious, he has continued to explore how pre-European-contact native peoples used resources at hand. "Limiting myself to the tools and materials available to primitive Americans," he has written, "would require me to rediscover ways of thinking and doing that had disappeared centuries ago, and would admit me into the world of the past." He has been doing the sugaring demonstration for the institute for over a decade and a half, as well as building longhouses, tools, and other objects. As much as any twenty-first-century person persisting in the mainstream, he has lived ancient practices. He's discovered much from wide reading, especially the observations of early French explorers and missionaries, but most of what he's learned has come from trial and error.

Dina's audience that cold March day was amazed that something so primitive could actually work and produce a useful product. They were equally amazed when he pulled out a small vial of dark, watery syrup and told them it was a day's work. "It's sweet," he said, but admitted it contained a bit of soot and dirt and had a burnt flavor from the hot rocks. Sometimes, he noted, Indians finished their syrup by simmering it over low fires in clay or birch-bark vessels. They also concentrated the sugar by letting the sap partially freeze and then discarding the ice, which is mostly water.

"It took all the knowledge and all the arms" when families moved to their sugar camps, writes Potawatomi tribal member and botany professor Robin Wall Kimmerer. It was "good storytelling time" until moments of furious activity when the "syrup reached just the right consistency" and "was beaten so that it would solidify in the desired way, into soft cakes, hard candy, and granulated sugar."

The origins of maple sugaring is lost to time and shrouded in mystery, a circumstance that only adds to its allure. Anyone walking in the late-winter woods has encountered icicles hanging from broken maple branches. How strange to think that such accomplished woodsmen as Native Americans would not have noticed and tasted the sweetness of these "sap-sickles" and drawn proper conclusions.

James Dina boiling sap Native American style

Acute observers of wildlife, they no doubt also watched squirrels nibbling at almost candy-like frozen drops of sap that had concentrated from evaporation and sublimation. Acclaimed naturalist Bernd Heinrich has seen red squirrels purposely making bite wounds in maple branches and returning at a later time when the sap had dried and thickened into a sugary residue. These animals "are not mere opportunistic exploiters of sap for drink but accomplished harvesters of maple sugar for food," he wrote in the February 1991 issue of *Natural History*. He concluded that humans might have learned to make syrup by observing these arboreal acrobats.

Embedded deep in Native American mythology is the cautionary tale that at first the creator made things too easy for people, and thick syrup flowed from trees all year. A deity encountered a lazy village of cold cooking fires, weed-bound gardens, and uncared-for children. He found the villagers in their sugar orchard, eyes closed and lying on their backs as sweet syrup dripped into their mouths. Enraged, the deity used his magical powers to dip a gigantic birch-bark bucket into a nearby lake and, rising above the trees, filled them with water until the syrup ran fast and thin. With the trees no longer directly providing a bounty of syrup, the tribe had to return to the hard work of hunting, fishing, and growing beans and corn. The hardest labor of all was reserved for making sugar from maple trees, and only at a time of year when no crops were available and game was scarce.

The earliest European observation of maple trees is often attributed to Jacques Cartier on his third voyage to Canada while exploring the St. Lawrence River in 1541. By 1557, the French monk André Thévet had written about the maple's sweet sap, and in 1606 Marc Lescarbot's *Histoire de la Nouvelle-France* described gathering and "distillation" of maple sap by Micmac Indians in eastern Canada. The dark, smoke-tinged, and often burnt-flavored sugar helped sustain natives in a lean time of year. With the advent of iron tools from Europe, much greater production efficiencies were achieved, and maple sugar became not only an article of subsistence but a market product driving further technological advances and social change.

· · · · · · ·

SOME SUGARHOUSES hang a kettle outside as a reminder of the colonial past. Museums have static exhibits displaying the big iron pots, and sometimes at festivals there are cauldrons actually boiling sap over roaring fires. But if you want to step back in time, however imperfectly, and find sugarmakers not only in period garb, but in period speech and attitude, there's probably no better place than Old Sturbridge Village in Sturbridge, Massachusetts, where each March they celebrate Maple Days circa 1830s. Sited on over two hundred acres, Old Sturbridge Village is the largest outdoor living history facility in the Northeast. Ensconced in a bucolic setting, this cluster of more than forty reproduction and historic buildings, some moved from other places in New England, features a town green surrounded by houses, a country store, a bank, and other businesses. There are farmsteads an easy walk outside the village, along with a gristmill, a sawmill, and a pottery with a large working kiln of brick. With just a little imagination, it's a place that causes you to step back.

My wife Mary and I entered this outdoor time machine on a blustery March day with a chill in the air but with sunlight strong enough to puddle and muddy the unpaved streets. Just off the town green and past a square fieldstone enclosure that was once a town pound for wayward animals, we walked carefully down a path paved in snow and gooey soil to where a burly, bearded young man was boiling sap over a roaring fire built beneath two large black iron kettles. The pots were suspended from a rough horizontal log strung between a boulder and an upright log with a forked crotch. Nearby, a hollow sumac twig was tapped into a twelve-inch maple and slowly dripped sap into a log trough at the base of the tree, a container not unlike the one James Dina used to boil sap.

Dressed in a knit wool cap and several layers of heavy, blousy shirts, the fellow frequently stoked the fire and ladled sap into the boiling kettles while we invaders from the twenty-first century gawked in our Thinsulate parkas and Gore-Tex hiking boots. He patiently answered questions no doubt heard hundreds of times. Bystanders asked about flavor, the amount of sap collected from a single tree, and how long it took to make a gallon of syrup (ten hours), though the lack of refrigeration or canning technology usually meant sugar, not syrup, was the end product. They were the same questions frequently posed to contemporary sugarmakers.

We left the kettles steaming, long tongues of orange flame licking the blackened metal, and made our way to a small, unpainted house where a tall, gray-haired man stood in front of a big fireplace. Using a small pot, he slowly heated and stirred syrup received from the large outdoor kettles until the sticky liquid nearly reached crystallization. At that point, the viscous syrup was poured into molds, where it hardened into a chunk of sugar. Two mottled brown lumps, one domed, one conical, stood before him on a table, the results of previous efforts. "This is how we make sugar," the docent said in a deep voice. "When we need some for our tea or baking, we chip off a piece."

Our final stop was the Freeman farmhouse on the village outskirts. In a kitchen crowded with visitors, a young woman in a bonnet and checked jumper stood in front of another huge fireplace as she baked tea-cake in a cast-iron Dutch oven. On a large table in front of her were doughnuts, squash pie, Indian pudding, and other delicacies, all sweetened with maple sugar. She was especially proud of the family's signature Brooks Cake. Filled with tart currents, it was also made with maple sugar. Invented by Mary Brooks, headmistress of the Concord, Massachusetts, Female Anti-Slavery Society, it was sold to raise funds for the cause and served at all Concord antislavery meetings. The docent had a soft, sweet voice, but she was adamant that we all use sugar made by free people rather than cane imported from the West Indies. Slave sugar, she called it.

* * * * * * *

MORAL DISTINCTIONS between maple and cane sugar developed more than a generation before the Civil War. Ever since, and for a variety of reasons, the use of maple products has not just been a matter of taste, but of politics as well. By the late 1780s, Quakers began promoting maple sugar as an alternative to the imperialist and slave-produced West Indian variety. In 1788, Philadelphia doctor and signer of the Declaration of Independence Benjamin Rush published an essay titled "Advantages of the Culture of the Sugar Maple Tree." The next year he and a group of Quakers formed a society for promoting maple sugar and staged a "scientific tea party" to prove the efficacy of the homegrown product. In a kind of taste-test focus group, Alexander Hamilton, prominent merchant Henry Drinker, and "several ladies" sipped cups of tea with like amounts of cane and maple sugar, all finding the maple just as sweet as its competitor.

Rush had known Thomas Jefferson since the Second Continental Congress, and in a letter of August 19, 1791, he wrote the future president that "I am led to expect that a material part of the general happiness which heaven seems to have prepared for mankind, will be derived from the manufacture and general use of Maple Sugar." By that time, Jefferson was already receptive, having purchased fifty pounds of maple sugar the previous autumn, not so much to fill his larder as to strike a blow against West Indian slavery. Jefferson was enthused by the possibilities of maple sugar, not only as a humanitarian cause, but as a means of cementing American commercial independence by encouraging the industry in frontier settlements.

The 1790s witnessed what has been called the "maple sugar bubble," a rising interest in maple production brought about by an odd alliance of abolitionists and land speculators with schemes to settle the frontier. Promotion of homegrown sugar by small landholders fit well with Jefferson's notion of yeoman farmer nobility, and a plentiful supply of sweetener free from tariffs and trade disruptions made a fine marriage of moral outrage and economic convenience. The bubble was fueled largely by New York real estate wheeler-dealers Arthur Noble and William Cooper, the father of novelist James Fenimore Cooper and the man for whom Cooperstown is named. They lured purchasers with unrealistic estimates of how much sugar could be produced by the land's trees, "these diamonds of America."

Regardless, maple sugar captured Jefferson's imagination, and a spring 1791 trip north found him proselytizing for planting maple orchards and sugar production. He even tried planting a sugar grove at Monticello, and on his way back home purchased sixty trees from a Long Island nursery. He met with little success, and by 1794 only eight saplings were alive. Two more trees were planted in 1798, and staff at Monticello speculate that a large maple still growing on the west lawn may be one of those. Though the maple bubble burst and his efforts to cultivate the tree at home failed, as late as 1808, toward the end of his second term as president, Jefferson still harbored hopes for the maple business. "I have never seen a reason," he wrote in a letter that summer, "why every farmer should not have a sugar orchard as well as an apple orchard. The supply of sugar for his family would require as little ground, and the process of making it as easy as that of cider."

The maple sugar bubble burst because of unreasonable estimates of capacity and settlers cutting many productive maples as they cleared acreage for crops and livestock. But the driving image that made the bubble possible, the concept of maple sugar as a patriotic product made by free and independent people working hard in the wholesome, natural atmosphere of the forest, had already been embedded in the culture and dates back to at least 1764, when Parliament passed the Sugar Act, not only raising import taxes on the American colonies, but damaging the colonial economy generally. The narrative of independence, wholesomeness, and hard work, first developed under British rule and in the early days of the Republic, has continued throughout our history and remains as part of maple syrup's allure today.

By 1810, wooden spouts inserted in holes made by augers were becoming popular and replacing the damaging gashing of trees that had been practiced since time immemorial. Sugarhouses had begun to appear by 1850, providing shelter in old-time sugar camps, though at first they were often primitive lean-tos. Just before the Civil War, as sheet metal was becoming widely manufactured, the first metal spouts were introduced, along with flat-bottom evaporator pans (providing more surface area for faster boiling) to replace kettles.

In 1860, American production reached its all-time peak, with forty million pounds of sugar and 1.6 million gallons of syrup. With emotions running high as the nation moved toward war over slavery, demand for maple sugar made by free men revived. Evaporating technology advanced quickly, with the first baffled pan to channel sap introduced in 1864, the two-pan system on a metal arch in 1872, metal sap-collection buckets in 1875, and pan bottoms corrugated into channels, known as flues, to increase heating surface in 1889. During the same period, the development of canning technology was at last a way of preserving syrup without having to reduce it to sugar

While technology advanced after the Civil War and made processing more efficient, consumer demand did not grow apace as cane sugar grew increasingly cheap with improved transportation and manufacturing methods. In 1818, maple sugar was half the price of cane, and by 1880 they were equal. By 1885, cane was cheaper for the first time. Maple continued to be consumed on farms and in rural regions, but price and easy availability, along with the notion that maple was outdated and old-fashioned, made cane the undisputed choice in growing urban areas.

While large maple packers buying vast quantities of syrup and acres of sugarbush, like the legendary Carey Maple Sugar Company of St. Johnsbury, Vermont, were on the rise in the late nineteenth century, their primary market was not ordinary households, but large food-processing corporations using maple as a flavoring. The tobacco industry was also a large user of maple sugar for enhancing both chewing and smoking products. Some of this maple syrup found its way into table syrups, even as these cane-based products reduced demand for the real thing. In the consumer's mind, maple syrup was relegated to a specialty topping for pancakes and waffles.

Consumer demand for maple syrup didn't rise again until World War II. Cane sugar supplies became limited, rationing was instituted, and interest in maple sugar became so great that government price controls were established limiting the charge per gallon to $3.39. Making maple syrup again became patriotic, a way to help feed the country and win the war.

·　·　·　·　·　·　·　·

NOW INTO THEIR seventies and eighties, Armand and Ernie Bolduc were sugaring as children during those war years. The land their Bolduc Farm is on has produced maple sugar since before Thomas Jefferson expressed any interest it. Sugaring has been a rite of spring on the Gilford, New Hampshire, property since at least 1779, making it the oldest continuous operation in the nation. Now a bit stooped and stiff, the men began sugaring at age four or five, helping collect sap with a gathering tank pulled by horses in snow that was deeper than they were tall. There is little money in their small-scale operation of under five hundred taps, all but ten buckets of which are on tubing, but sugaring is in their blood, and they take joy in carrying on a long, unbroken tradition. The arch into which they toss chunks of wood was made in the 1870s.

The brothers delight in introducing school groups to the mysteries of maple, especially kids in the local Head Start program. The sugarhouse walls are decorated with drawings, photos, and thank-you notes from their youthful fans. In a good year the Bolducs make about ninety gallons of syrup.

The sugarhouse is a cozy, low building sheathed in weathered shingles and sporting a classic cupola rising above a metal roof. Built in 1983, it replaced a much older structure up the hill, parts of which may date from the eighteenth century. The old barn-board building sits in the midst of the maple grove, a little lopsided, the roof picturesquely rusting. Unwilling to see the venerable sugar shack suffer demolition by neglect, the Bolducs restored it about a decade ago, replacing rotten siding and sills and giving it concrete footings. Marked by generations of use and repair, it's now a storehouse for old equipment. No one knows how much of the building is original, though undoubtedly it partakes of four centuries of imagination and hard work.

The farm itself got its start in the 1770s when the land was settled by the prominent Jewett family, according to a short typescript history written by the Reverend Hector Bolduc, Armand and Ernie's brother. The Jewetts not only ran the farm, but operated a tavern and country store. Benjamin Jewett was postmaster, justice of the peace, and held other positions of authority. The farm produced several pounds of maple sugar in 1779, according to his diary. Later he mentions "trading two pounds of maple sugar to Gove the blacksmith for four pounds of nails."

Sugaring on the farm began out of doors. The Jewetts would "suspend a large kettle from a 'green wood' tripod and keep a hot fire of 'pine knots glowing' beneath." Later they built a lean-to covered with pine and fir boughs to protect the kettle and fire from the elements.

Ernie and Armand treat their trees with reverence and take pains to care for them by keeping the brush down and practicing proper thinning. Walking the sun-drenched woods with them, to a visitor it seemed that every tree of any size bred stories or had family associations. The Bolduc sugarbush was long reputed to be the sweetest in Belknap County, they said. The sap was so rich that someone once accused their father of dosing it with cane sugar; their dad was "furious." Agricultural agents and farmers debated the issue for years. "No conclusive verdict was ever reached," Hector wrote, "but it was finally determined that it was most likely caused by the fact that the Bolduc's dairy herd was pastured each night in the maple orchard." Manure deposited over the years had fertilized the soil, resulting in sweeter trees, some observers concluded.

In the 1950s, the state built a highway bypass through the middle of the sugarbush. The Bolducs fought the road vigorously, but eminent domain triumphed, and all but a hundred of their five hundred trees, some five to six feet in diameter at the stump, were lost. Road salt continues to slowly kill some of those that remain. On the day crews arrived with bulldozers and chainsaws, the brothers' father watched from the farmhouse door. Tears cascaded down his cheeks as he watched "one after another of his trees die." He was devastated. It was the only time his boys saw him cry. Though they are gentle folk and it happened decades ago, there's hint of bitterness in Ernie and Armand's voices when they describe the loss of the trees to macadam.

The brothers' father liked to inaugurate the season with a sugaring-off party. Friends, neighbors, and relatives would gather to watch hot syrup poured over fresh snow. When it cooled, they would twirl the taffy-like confection around wooden spoons and delight in the chewy texture and maple flavor. One time, they said, a boy grabbed the sticky candy with a woollen mitten and immediately became barehanded to peals of laughter. An adult once had his false teeth dislodged. Children would receive slivers of bread with syrup poured over them, while "the men liked to gather around the small pan of hot syrup set on a stand outside the sugar house and mix scrambled eggs into the hot syrup. It was not unusual to mix a quantity of whisky or brandy with this mixture for added flavor."

If you stop by the sugarhouse at Bolduc Farm when the sap is flowing, you're likely to be served a dinner-plate-size flapjack with maple syrup hot off the evaporator, just for the asking. Sometimes there's also a side of kielbasa or bacon, but always there are heaping portions of genial hospitality and stories that delight even more than the food.

Sugaring teaches that "Mother Nature is boss," Armand said, hands in the pockets of his worn overalls. He pulled them out and adjusted his cap. "We get volunteer helpers who are like family, but real apprentices are hard to come by. I hope we'll be able to continue the tradition, but it will be tough."

* * * * * * *

PERHAPS MORE THAN other farmers, or makers of any other product, for that matter, maple people have a keen sense of the past. They value their heritage. Few are without their prized sugaring antiques, and many, like Alvin and David Clark, Mike Girard, Russ Davenport of Shelburne, Massachusetts, and Rick Marsh of Jeffersonville, Vermont, have turned their sugarhouses or retail outlets into mini-museums. Even those with the latest, most technically sophisticated equipment are collectors. From the mists of Native American oral traditions to the electronics of today, they feel linked to their history and willingly spill stories resonating with the past even as they concentrate their vacuum-sucked sap with RO and run it through oil-fired evaporators.

Maple is a thread that tells a story in the larger fabric of American life. It throws the transformation of our culture into high relief because it's the same centuries-old product produced using radically new means. Sugarmakers often revel in the changes they've seen, not necessarily out of nostalgia, but in recognition of the role they play in advancing the times.

The octogenarian Davenport, one of the most award-winning and celebrated sugarmakers in the country, gladly tells visitors how his grandfather showed him the way to create a spout by burning the soft pith from a sumac twig with a hot wire. "Just in my lifetime," he has written, "I have gone from oxen to horses, tractors, trucks, and an ATV as a means of working in the sugarbush. From bit-brace to chain-saw drills, to backpack 'tappers,' to battery powered drills, to cord-less 18-volt drills the task of tapping has become more up-to-date." While his son Norman or his grandson Fred tends the evaporator, the grizzled veteran of many maple seasons with his thick mustache and soft blue eyes eagerly tells visitors how he remembers a wood-stave gathering tank pulled by oxen on a sled, and early experiments with his friend, tubing inventor Bob Lamb. Filtering, he told me with a smile, has gone from old flannel bedsheets to machines filled with diatomaceous earth.

Displayed throughout the sugarhouse, Davenport's array of an-tiques, from buckets to sugar molds, spiles, and tubing, is impressive. Nevertheless, a sign near the collection advertises his interest in pur-chasing more. People like Davenport don't just talk about sugaring history, they've lived it. "In my lifetime," he notes, "maple sugaring has seen more progress than in the hundreds of years during the early life of mankind's involvement in this process."

The maple sugar narrative established in the eighteenth century still resonates. Syrup continues to symbolize independence, whole-someness, and the hard work of free people. Specific manifestations of that story have changed, but the underlying principles remain. Sugar-makers are clearly proud of their heritage and believe in it, but it is also good as an engine of product sales and tourism. It's a narrative that vibrates with longing for a golden New England past, a kind of *Yankee Magazine* yearning for simpler times.

Maple has always had a role in recurring back-to-the-land move-ments, manifest most commonly today in a desire for what is organic and sustainable. It's tied to our reverence for trees and twenty-first-century interest in the regenerated forests of the region. Colonial-era passions of resistance and a desire for independence find expression through consumer interest in locally grown products more healthful than what are offered by multinational industrial food corporations. Using maple is a kind of insurgency against such corporate authority, a reflection of desire for more control over our bodies. Maple producers, even the large players, are small compared to the purveyors of other sweeteners. Decentralized production feeds the hunger for local products. This locavore movement favoring artisanal foods is a direct descendant of Jefferson's faith and love for small yeoman farmers.

Sugaring is fused with New England identity and culture, as rooted in this region as Bunker Hill, lobster, Plymouth Rock, and Thanksgiving. Though technology has taken us far, probably no ancient Native American tradition of the eastern woodlands is still so widely practiced as sugaring. The past is still present in every sugarhouse.

Roast Chickens with Black Pepper-Maple Glaze

Yield: 6 servings

INGREDIENTS

2 tablespoons unsalted butter
½ cup maple syrup
Coarsely ground pepper
2 medium onions, halved lengthwise and thinly sliced crosswise
2 teaspoons extra-virgin olive oil
Salt
Two 3½-pound organic chickens

DIRECTIONS

1. Preheat the oven to 350°F.
2. In a small saucepan, melt the butter with the maple syrup and 2 teaspoons of coarsely ground pepper. Remove the glaze from the heat.
3. On a large heavy-duty rimmed baking sheet, toss the sliced onions with the olive oil. Season the onions with salt and pepper and spread in an even layer.
4. Season the chickens inside and out with salt. Truss chickens loosely and then arrange them on top of the onions.
5. Roast the chickens for 15 minutes.
6. Brush the chickens all over with half of the maple glaze and continue roasting them for 1 hour longer.
7. Increase the oven temperature to 425°F. Generously brush the chickens with the remaining glaze and roast for 15 minutes more, or until the cavity juices run clear and the chickens are richly browned.
8. Transfer the chickens to a platter and let rest for 10 minutes before carving.
9. Pour the onions and pan juices into a large glass measuring cup and skim the fat from the surface. Season with salt and pepper and serve with the chickens.

Recipe by Anna Gill

Maple Cupcakes

Yield: 18 cupcakes

INGREDIENTS

2½ cups all-purpose flour

2 teaspoons baking powder

1 teaspoon baking soda

½ teaspoon salt

¼ teaspoon ground ginger

1 stick unsalted butter, softened

½ cup packed light-brown sugar

2 eggs

1¼ cups maple syrup

2 teaspoons vanilla extract

½ cup buttermilk

½ cup walnuts or pecans, finely chopped

Maple-butter frosting, recipe below

DIRECTIONS

1. Preheat the oven to 350°F.
2. Sift together the dry ingredients (flour through ginger) and set aside.
3. Beat the butter and brown sugar together until fluffy.
4. Add in the eggs, maple syrup, and vanilla extract and beat well.
5. Stir in the flour mixture by thirds, alternating with the buttermilk.
6. Mix in the nuts.
7. Fill 18 paper-lined muffin cups and bake until cake tester comes out clean, about 20 minutes.
8. Cool completely, then top with maple-butter frosting.

Maple-Butter Frosting

INGREDIENTS

3 tablespoons butter, softened

1¾ cups confectionary sugar

¼ teaspoon vanilla extract

¼ teaspoon maple syrup

To make the frosting, combine all the ingredients together and beat well to mix.

Recipe by Shirley Hewlett

Yankee Ingenuity

IS THERE ANY food production process simpler or more monotonous than a sugarmaker's task of boiling? And if you think watching paint dry or grass grow might be dull, maybe you haven't heard that a watched pot never boils. Of course, any sugarmaker knows that despite hawk-like observation, the pot, or evaporator, does eventually boil. The problem arises with the thrill of a massive sap run generating endless gallons that boil and boil and boil seemingly forever in a profligate expenditure of time and fuel. Old-timers like Wilson "Bill" Clark, a silver-haired man who was president of the Vermont Maple Sugar Makers Association for more than thirty years, recall days of backbreaking, nonstop boiling like 1968 when he went over ninety-five hours with just three hours down for a middle-of-the-night fuel oil delivery. So while necessity is often touted as the mother of invention in most endeavors, for sugarmakers it's a combination of exhaustion and long hours watching boiling sap that drives new ideas for efficiencies.

Of all occupations, maple sugaring probably has the most laymen per capita who think like scientists, because time spent quietly boiling with not much else to do begets observations that produce questions often leading to research and invention, notes Dr. Perkins of the Proctor Center. "Sugarmakers are innovators," Burr Morse writes. "Heavy, sloshing gathering buckets and deep snow begs creativity." Or, as Bruce Bascom puts it, "maple people do not sit still. They're always tinkering."

You wouldn't think that such a simple process, especially one with an old-timey image and cherished history, could be a paradigm of innovation, but when an antsy sugarmaker confronts the confluence of nature's unpredictability and an adaptable technique, the result is ingenuity. Sure, you're likely to see a few galvanized buckets hanging from a tree near the door to a sugarhouse, but most sugarmakers of any size put them out just to attract trade and keep the old-fashioned image alive in the customer's mind. The true icons of contemporary maple are vacuum tubing and RO machines. Perhaps no food so natural and easily made has undergone such an extensive technical revolution in production.

But for tubing, the Bolduc brothers would not have been making syrup into and beyond their seventies, at least not without a lot of help that likely would have been prohibitively expensive. The typical sixteen-quart bucket weighs over thirty pounds when full. Even if half full, five hundred buckets would require lifting over seven thousand pounds every time there was a decent sap run, a bit much for even a vigorous septuagenarian. Instead, being cagey New Englanders, they moved their sugarhouse down low by the road and let gravity deliver sap straight to their sugarhouse. The move also pleased the gregarious pair with an increased likelihood of visitors.

"Tubing saved the entire maple industry," Bruce Bascom told me on a 2009 visit to the cluster of buildings that comprise his hilltop home, sugarhouse, syrup storage facility, and equipment showroom in southwestern New Hampshire. Without tubing, the cost of production would have become so high that maple syrup might have been relegated to an exotic and expensive specialty product with limited appeal, like truffle oil or caviar.

Bruce and I left behind a warren of offices and entered the spacious production floor where a worker handed us light-blue hairnets. Now in his sixties, Bruce was in high school when practical tubing came out. He stopped us at a bar chart illustrating production going back to 1954. "It's a third of the way through the season, and we've made just under half of last year's crop," he said, pointing to the wall. Dressed in baggy khakis and a flannel shirt with tails hanging out, Bruce is a fast-talking self-described maple fanatic with a Cheshire cat smile. He had eighty-one thousand of his own taps in 2014 and another twelve thousand of purchased sap, but what distinguishes his business from that of most large producers is the volume of other peoples' syrup he buys and sells. He gets it by the tractor-trailer load and has millions of pounds in storage. Bulk syrup is measured by weight, with a gallon weighing eleven pounds.

Facts and figures easily poured out of Bruce. He knew who was up and who was down, who was boiling and who couldn't get into the woods because of deep snow. He does little hands-on sugaring anymore, spending his time putting together business deals. Sugaring attracts a certain kind of gambler, is an outlet for risk, he told me. Sugarmakers get a thrill out of unpredictability, the odds of making as much syrup as they did the year before or the year before that. "It's no fun winning," he repeated a few times, "if you can't lose."

"Buckets were labor intensive, and labor is expensive," he said. "One person with tubing can do what five or ten with buckets can." But perfecting tubing didn't come easily. It was trial and error in the early days, both in setup and materials. After much frustration, Bruce's father Ken threw out his first tubing because it cracked and wouldn't straighten.

Bruce claims to have the largest inventory of used and new equipment in the country, and sooner or later a sugarmaker within a day's drive is likely to find himself in the large, well-lit store with its gleaming evaporators, rolls of bright tubing, stacks of buckets, fittings of every kind, signs, labels, containers, and anything else a maple person might need or desire. If you want to try a new piece of technology, you're likely to find it here. "Our customers are not normal people," Bruce said affectionately. "Maple producers are deviants because they want to work hard, have a hands-on experience, be their own boss, and place bets with Mother Nature."

A trip to this super-center of sugaring was an annual pilgrimage for me back in the days when I made syrup. I bought used buckets and spiles, a plastic storage tank, hydrometers, felt and paper filters, flue brushes, pan cleaner, and a host of other supplies. I was like a kid in a candy store and always came home with more than I intended to buy. A shrewd businessman unafraid to speak his mind on general industry matters, Bruce keeps his syrup dealings close to the vest like all the big players. Still, this giant of the sugaring world with a boyish face that belies his age is free with his knowledge, welcoming and helpful to those who share his passion. With an estimated sixteen thousand customers, Bruce is influential not just because of the scale of his business and his experience, but because of his contact with so many other sugarmakers, large and small, who buy equipment and syrup from him.

Bascom Maple Farms is located a little north of Keene in Acworth, New Hampshire. It's a rugged land of uneven hills and twisting roads with frost heaves akin to ski slope moguls. The woods are always close and often strung with a cat's cradle of soft blue tubing. Old galvanized stock tanks and large plastic containers collect sap at the pavement's edge. Sugarhouses are tucked along roadsides or up long dirt drives.

It's a long climb up Sugar House Road to the burst of light and space near the top of Mount Kingsbury where a complex of dark-brown, barnlike buildings is perched near a handsome stone house where Bruce lives. The hired man lived there when Bruce was a kid. He grew up just downslope in a house his father built. The view is expansive, and the eye carries across sloping fields to thick hardwood forests punctuated by evergreens and then to distant mountains. In 2012, he added a large two-story rectangular building with twenty-two thousand square feet on each floor and three loading docks. The first floor stores seven and a half million gallons of syrup in drums. The second floor has a bottling line, offices, and storage.

Bascoms started sugaring here in 1853. As late as the early 1960s, when he was in grammar school, Bruce remembers going out with his dad across a snowy field in a wagon laden with sap buckets drawn by draft horses. They had about six thousand galvanized buckets in those days, and cleaning them was backbreaking work. Ken Bascom, who was a director and president of the North American Maple Syrup Council, was a creative tinkerer and invented an outdoor steam-powered bucket washer. Bruce describes his dad as a workaholic tyrant who was enthralled with anything maple. They were partners for twenty-five years and often communicated by shouting at each other. Toward the end of his life, Ken was asked how he liked working with his son. "Ever tried riding a runaway horse?" he responded.

• • • • • • •

METAL TUBING for sugaring was developed in 1916 by W. C. Brower of Mayfield, New York. It was still being used in a few places as late as the 1950s. Jody Bronson says Great Mountain Forest used an "in-

A cat's cradle of tubing

tricate maze of aluminum pipe" whereby sap could be poured from hillside dumping stations to a large holding tank near the sugar-house. While the concept was good, metal proved impractical because of night freezing, leakage, and damage by roaming deer.

Plastic tubing was patented by Nelson Griggs of Montpelier, Vermont, in 1959 just as several others were also at work perfecting the technology. They confronted issues such as appropriate diameter; whether they should use colors that would warm the sap to get it flowing or keep it cool to prevent bacterial growth; expansion and contraction with temperature change; durability; sag resistance; flexibility; and other concerns. Among the pioneers was Bob Lamb from upstate New York, some of whose early experiments in a vintage Quonset hut were with surgical tubing. Lamb has been described as tall, soft-spoken, and quiet. He was both entrepreneurial and inventive. "He always seemed to have a better idea for just about everything," Mike Girard told me. Lamb's name became the most widely recognized in the business, and tubing bearing his moniker is still sold.

Some sugarmakers, as Burr Morse recalls, felt like guinea pigs for the plastics manufacturers, and he remembers the many common mistakes he and his dad made when they first strung tubing in 1975. Sometimes they had to reconstruct the system so laboriously laid out, and in really bad cases temporarily reverted to buckets. It took three years to plumb three thousand taps.

Tubing at last enabled sugarmakers to find advantage in one of New England's most pervasive natural resources, its hilly terrain. It took producers from the equivalent of dipping pails in a well to indoor plumbing in just a few years. By the late 1970s, few operations of any size relied principally on buckets. Tubing not only brought sap directly from the tree to the sugarhouse or a large roadside container where it could easily be pumped into a truck; it opened areas to production that were previously inaccessible because of ravines, stream crossings, and other geographical features, or that were simply too remote. It also limited the need for vehicles in the sugarbush, reducing damage to trees from mechanical injury and soil compaction. Because it brought a lot of good used buckets onto the market at a reasonable price, tubing was also good for small producers like me who weren't ever going to try it.

Although some producers who have converted to tubing say they miss the way buckets enabled them to know the sap flow habits of individual trees, sap moving through tubing gives a kinetic, visual sense of flow, which in a way is what sap collection is all about. Because laying out a tubing system, whether vacuum or gravity, requires careful evaluation of the land's topography, it also can provide a more comprehensive understanding of the landscape than that gained by regularly trudging over rough, sloping ground emptying buckets. Some people think that tubing gives too much of an industrial appearance to the woods, but I look at the lines like celebratory ribbons or akin to Tibetan prayer flags in their various shades of gray, green, blue, black, and purple. Few realize that the galvanized buckets we feel nostalgia for today were once a source of complaint as they replaced wooden stave buckets because they also appeared too industrial and it was felt they would heat up in sunlight and spoil sap. But metal proved easier to carry, store, and clean, and wooden buckets soon disappeared.

Technology has moved so fast that you can forgive traditional sugarmakers for a bit of resistance from future shock or historical whiplash. Burr Morse tells of an elderly sugarmaker who was finally persuaded to install tubing after years of resistance. He did his best stringing lines through the woods, but installed most of it poorly and got only about one-third his normal crop. After the season, he pulled the plastic down and trashed it, swearing he'd rather die collecting with buckets than use tubing again. "By God he did, too," Morse relates, "dropped right in his tracks the next season. Spilt two gathering pails of good sap when he keeled over!"

"A tubing system is comprised of a network of plastic lines of various diameters, resembling a number of small streams flowing into a larger river and ultimately to a reservoir," instructs the *North American Maple Syrup Producers Manual.* Spouts tapped into the tree are attached to narrow drop lines that connect to five-sixteenths-inch lateral lines passing from tree to tree. The laterals connect to three-quarter-inch or larger main lines, which in some sugar orchards flow into even bigger main lines called conductors. The main lines bring sap to storage tanks. Generally, storage tanks are at a low point, but depending on topography, some sap may be assisted with pumps.

There's a lot of technique to installing tubing, and while the old mantra of "straight, tight, and sloping continuously downhill" still makes sense, vacuum systems and pumps make it possible to plumb even complex geography. I've seen sugarmakers installing systems not only with the aid of detailed maps and GPS devices, but surveyor's rods and transits. The shape of drop lines to prevent pooling sap, length of lateral lines and configuration, type of connectors and other hardware, line tension, and support wires are among many considerations when rigging tubing.

Installation is only the beginning of the work. Tubing requires continual vigilance and patrolling. Falling tree branches are a constant hazard, and there are even cases of entangled deer or moose. Wind and ice damage are also possibilities. One of the biggest problems is one of nature's smaller creatures. Suburbanites may rail at acrobatic squirrels stealing sunflower seeds from a bird feeder, but it's nothing compared to the expletives a sugarmaker may utter at their woodland cousins chewing tubing. Burr Morse complains that the furry critters may attack every tree, munch randomly, or even take plastic spouts to their cache.

Bascom's catalog devotes more pages to tubing systems than any other product, including evaporators. Not only are coils of drop, lateral, and main line illustrated, but spouts, supports, clamps, tension grips, connectors, tees, elbows, plugs, reducers, couplings, and many other accessories. Several pages past the tubing are a few types of increasingly necessary vacuum pumps and all the tackle that goes with them— regulators, gauges, and releasers also called extractors (which separate air from liquid in the lines, enabling sap to drain into collection tanks).

Vacuum was first employed in the early days of tubing as dairy farmers who also sugared experimented with pumps used to get milk from cow udders. These pumps reached about fifteen inHg (inches of mercury), though ones achieving twenty-five inHg are now common. University of Vermont researchers have found that an additional inch of vacuum at the taphole raises sap yields 5 to 7 percent. It's increasingly rare to find producers of any size and even some small ones who don't put vacuum on their tubing.

Armand Bolduc shook his head when I asked about vacuum. "In the long term, trees won't put up with it," he said pointedly. "You can't screw around with Mother Nature." But Tim Perkins's research has shown no appreciable difference in health among trees on gravity, low, or high vacuum. He recommends the highest pressure you can get for the best sap yields.

‧ ‧ ‧ ‧ ‧ ‧ ‧ ‧

I WAS TALKING about vacuum with Bruce as we passed through a spacious area filled with pallets of syrup ready for shipment. Some held square cardboard containers with interior plastic bladders holding 220 gallons. "Better than drums because they cost less and they're easy to recycle," he said, catching my glance. "It's crazy not to use vacuum," he told me, changing the subject back, "when it so dramatically improves yields." By lowering pressure in the tubing, he explained, sap flows from higher pressure within the tree to lower pressure at the spout. Sap will come as long as temperatures remain above freezing. "Vacuum also keeps bacteria out of tapholes and makes them less likely to dry out."

Soon we were among the bottling lines where containers are filled, capped, and labeled via a series of conveyors and revolving trays.

Workers were busy packing jugs in corrugated boxes. I suggested vacuum as a way to temporarily stem the impact of global warming. Bruce shrugged and told me about a drug dog on the Canadian border that was attracted to a container that was sticky on the outside. Of course, the drum had to be inspected. Afterward, the cover was not replaced tightly, and by the time he got home there were gallons of syrup sloshing in the back of the truck. "It was a mess. I guess German shepherds like maple."

Vacuum has become the heart of many sugarbush circulatory systems and indeed provides a technical solution for producing sap even during prolonged warm spells before buds break on the trees. "Buying a good vacuum pump," Cornell's Dr. Michael Farrell states in *The Sugarmaker's Companion*, "is probably the best insurance policy you can get for a changing climate." Because vacuum requires fewer taps than gravity systems and can obtain comparable yields from smaller tapholes, it may also reduce stress on trees.

Bruce was talking about bills of lading and bar codes as we approached the evaporator. Interrupted several times for calls, he took them at a wall phone on the production floor. The evaporator is four feet wide by twelve feet long and fitted with a Steam-Away, a stainless hood that fits over the unit and uses heat in rising vapor to warm oncoming sap and remove water before it enters the evaporator pan. The sap is heated with steam pipes at 325 degrees Fahrenheit using an oil-fired boiler in the basement. It's an unusual arrangement, which Bruce's father pioneered. "Steam heats evenly, and you can't burn the syrup," he said proudly. In most places, the evaporator is the centerpiece of the sugarhouse. At Bascom's, it's off to the side. Not an afterthought, to be sure, but clearly not the main event either.

Oil is efficient, and all the larger operators use it, Bruce told me. Although only a quarter of producers are on oil, three-quarters of the syrup is made with it. "Wood may be cheaper in some respects, but the logistics and labor of handling it make it hard." Having visited several sugarhouses along the Canadian border in Somerset County, Maine, where very few operations have fewer than ten thousand taps and oil is the fuel of choice, I knew Bruce was right.

Few consumers think of syrup as being made with oil-fired rigs, but for sugarmakers it has advantages. With a flip of a switch it turns on and off quickly, allowing a more instantaneous and controlled boil. Sugarmakers of any size who pay for labor find oil less expensive. Of course, there's not much romance in firing with oil or the good feeling that comes from using a local product and renewable resource that can be harvested in the sugarbush and encourages good forest management. Sugarhouses with lots of visitors often prefer wood for its aesthetics, warmth, and classic image. Despite the environmental damage caused in producing and burning fossil fuels, Farrell concludes that "because larger operations that burn fuel oil remove the vast majority of the water through reverse osmosis before the sap is boiled, they can actually have a lower carbon footprint than smaller, hobby-sized operations boiling raw sap by burning wood."

Bruce escorted me into a small room tangled with a network of plastic and copper pipes. Valves and tanks were labeled, and several electrical boxes hung on the walls. It seemed more complicated than the plumbing of a city fire pumper. At the far end of the space was a Springtech Elite 3200 reverse osmosis machine, an off-white rectangular box stippled with dials and gauges above a row of tubular glass flow meters. There were buttons and switches. Behind it were steel cylinders containing the semi-permeable membranes by which water is removed from sap. "This is the only economical way to produce syrup today," Bruce said, folding his hands on his chest. "And it's 'green,' because with RO the amount of wood or oil used to boil is dramatically reduced." Bruce's father installed the first RO in New Hampshire.

Where tubing saved commercial sugaring by reducing labor costs, RO has rescued it from escalating fuel prices. Originally designed for seawater desalinization, RO has been used in the maple industry since the 1970s to concentrate the sugar content of sap before boiling. RO machines pressurize sap and force it through membranes with pores that allow water to pass but are too small for bigger sugar molecules. RO can save not only fuel but also time, reducing boiling by as much as 75 to 85 percent. Straight from the tree, sap of 2 percent sugar content requires forty-three gallons of sap to make one gallon of syrup. An RO concentrating sap to 8 percent sugar takes less than eleven gallons to make a gallon of syrup, reducing boiling time by about 75 percent. Double the concentrate to 16 percent and it takes less than five and a half gallons to make a gallon of syrup. The highest sugar content that producers are bringing sap to is about 22 percent, taking less than four gallons of concentrate to make a gallon of syrup.

It once took about four gallons of fuel oil to make a gallon of syrup, but with RO the amount of oil per gallon of syrup is less than one and sometimes less than one-half. RO enables sugarmakers to increase the number of taps while downsizing evaporators, a contradiction little more than a generation ago. It also makes it feasible to tap less-sugary red maples, a common tree in many areas. All this can result in cost savings. Of course, gone is the exhausting romance of two- or three-day continuous boils, something that always seemed better in later telling than it was at the time.

The idea behind RO, removing water from sap without boiling, is as old as tossing pieces of ice out of buckets. But the high-tech technique has changed the maple industry beyond a new way of concentrating sugar. Its cost has sharpened the divide between small and large producers, making it increasingly hard for part-time operations to survive. Farrell estimates that at least five hundred taps are necessary for RO to make sense economically, since even small "hobby" models cost around $7,000. Larger machines listed in Bascom's catalog are the only items labeled "prices upon request." Of course, hobbyists or small producers with mechanical and plumbing skills can cut costs dramatically by making their own RO or retrofitting one that has been used for water purification

Some operators who get a lot of visitors don't use RO because their customers want to see sap boiling. It's especially true of educational institutions where maximizing syrup production is not the principal aim. When Coolwater Sugarhouse was a commercial operation in the early 1970s, Great Mountain Forest had one of the first RO machines in Connecticut, Jody Bronson recalls. Reconstituted as a nonprofit forestry and ecology learning center, they've reduced the amount of syrup they make and forgone not only RO but steam hoods and other innovations that cloak the process. "We want folks to experience not only something they can taste, but see, hear, smell, and touch," Bronson insists.

Bruce arched an eyebrow and flashed his trademark impish grin. "RO is usually hidden from public view," he said. "It's not much in the traditional image. Not that it's secret, but the public just doesn't ask. Besides, the machines can't be allowed to freeze, and a small, closed room is easier to heat." Heat, electricity, and sophisticated plumbing are all problematic for small producers, he acknowledged.

Controversy remains over whether RO affects flavor, since syrup's distinctive characteristics come from caramelizing sugars during boiling. Some producers deride "techno-syrup" as having too little taste, though their number is declining as RO is increasingly used. Of course, people long for the bygone flavors they grew up with. "We may as well confess," wrote Cornell University professor Anna Botsford Comstock in 1911 about the conversion from the "old caldron kettle" to "new fangled sugar-houses" with evaporators, "that the maple sirup of today seems to us a pale and anemic liquid, lacking the delicious flavor of the rich, dark nectar which we, with the help of cinders, smoke and various other things, brewed of yore in the open woods."

As we walked into the well-lit showroom buzzing with customers even on this November day distant from sugaring season, I asked Bruce if he thinks RO changes syrup flavor. He stopped and leaned against a counter faced with maple boards stained with dark dots and long streaks from years of tapping when they were still part of living trees. At a concentration of 8 percent sugar, there's no difference, he assured me with a wave of his hand. Higher concentrations, he said, yield lighter, milder syrup. He paused and, ever the salesman, added, "but that's what a lot of customers want, especially bulk buyers."

Under Dr. Perkins's guidance, the Proctor Center conducted tests in 2008 and 2009 using RO-processed sap at various sugar concentrations. They boiled the samples under like conditions using sap from various points in the season. Examining the resulting syrup for physiochemical factors (pH, density, color, and conductivity), chemical elements like minerals, and volatile flavor and aromatic compounds, the scientists detected differences in some properties, including flavor compounds. However, these differences were undetectable to people in sensory test trials. Just as Bruce told me, the only significant distinction between syrup made from high-concentration RO sap and less sweet sap is that higher concentrates tend to produce lighter syrups.

Regardless of the bulk market where Bruce does most of his business, many sugarmakers have customers who increasingly favor darker, more robust, and full-flavored syrup. While light-syrup advocates call the ro-processed product delicate and subtle, those who prefer bigger flavor see it as bland and lacking character. Though it's doubtful dark-syrup advocates share Professor Comstock's lament for the smoke-and-cinder days of kettle boiling, the vagaries of taste will likely continue to fuel controversy about ro. Nevertheless, many people feel the environmental benefits of ro trump any change in flavor, especially since most syrup today is blended to please a range of tastes.

Bruce led me outside and into a concrete-bunker-like building with interior walls of uneven foam insulation. It was stacked with barrels, old food drums, and even beer kegs filled with syrup. Bruce talked about different container shapes, the advantages of metal or plastic, the gauge of various materials, how long they lasted, and their ease of cleaning as we walked past them and into a narrow refrigerated room with several stainless-steel silos, each containing thousands of gallons. This is over a million dollars' worth of syrup when full, he said, and then told me about the additional storage building he was planning.

Bruce reached into his pocket and pulled out small piece of plastic. "They say this tiny technology is going to generate more syrup, even when conditions are not best," he said. "Some people think check-valve spouts are potentially as revolutionary as tubing, vacuum, and ro. Time will tell. They're cheap, and you're best off buying new ones each year. We're moving more every season. I've got to make some calls, but on your way out take a look in the store. Of course, the technology keeps changing, and I like to hedge my bets. We use four or five kinds of spouts."

Bruce left, and I returned to the showroom, where thousands of the innovative taps could be purchased. Check-valve spouts allow sterile sap to flow out of the tree but prevent any liquid, which may be contaminated with bacteria, from flowing back when the pressure gradient reverses. A tiny ball inside the spout is pushed away from the tree when sap flows, but when it stops running, negative pressure sucks the ball back, where it seats against a ring, blocking backward flow. By reducing bacteria and yeast growth, the valves keep tapholes from drying out and healing as quickly as they do with a conventional spile, thus enabling a longer season. When the valves are used with vacuum systems, yields may increase by as much as 75 percent, maple equipment manufacturer Leader Evaporator claims, and up to 47 percent in sugarbushes dependent on gravity. It seemed astounding. I decided to head a little north of Burlington, Vermont, where I visited Leader in its sprawling, boxy industrial-park building just outside Swanton, a short drive from Canada.

· · · · · · · ·

LEADER IS A venerable company that had its start in Enosburg Falls, Vermont, in 1888. Since the 1960s, it has bought out other maple equipment manufacturers and is now the largest business of its kind in the United States. In its current location since 2006, it has forty-five thousand square feet of manufacturing space and thirty-five thousand for a store and showroom.

I met soft-spoken Fred Petig in a small reception area among a cluster of offices. He took me down a short corridor that opened into a vast hangar-like area with a spacious showroom full of gleaming stainless-steel evaporators, RO machines, filter presses, vacuum pumps, and spool after spool of blue lateral and black mainline tubing. A large wall displayed sugaring antiques. Sales have increased dramatically over the past few years with the advent of new technology and food safety standards, Petig said. He showed me a new touch-screen RO while explaining that concentrating sap has also meant a resurgence in evaporator sales as many producers downsize with the need for less boiling.

Beyond the sales area, metalworking occupied most of the building, including bending, cutting, and welding by men with rough hands wearing ball caps, jeans, and heavy boots. Much of the work remains done by hand, albeit with some high-tech tools. I was shown a new computer-driven, laser sheet-metal cutter; devices designed to bend steel; and a series of welding booths separated by red plastic strips. An extrusion line snaked out 150 feet of lateral tubing per minute from tiny plastic pellets.

Though other items in Leader's line were bigger, more complex or impressive, it was the tiny check valve that Petig was most excited about. An injection-molded product, it was made off-site to company specifications by a nearby subcontractor.

In the fall of 2007, Dr. Perkins and his staff began work on creating a practical check-valve spout and tested the prototype to promising results the next season. In the fall of 2008, Leader and the Proctor Center signed an agreement allowing for cooperative research and testing to develop a commercial product. Together they created a design and made a pattern for a check-valve spout adapter that attached to so-called stubby spouts. Produced in limited quantities for testing at Proctor and by select sugarmakers in the 2009 season, it met with substantial success. By 2012, the adapters, as well clear polycarbonate check-valve spouts, were becoming increasingly popular.

Petig was proud of the public-private partnership that developed the check valve. The tiny plastic spile would help with problems caused by erratic and warmer weather. If tapholes don't heal so quickly and stop the flow of sap, then the disadvantage of tapping early is reduced, and later sap runs won't be curtailed because of yeast and bacteria. "It's the future of tapping," Petig grinned, echoing the company's catalog boast.

Delaying the tree's natural wound response to increase sap flow has long been a goal of syrup producers. Forty years earlier there was some use of a chemical called paraformaldehyde. It was somewhat successful but raised issues of tree health and chemical contamination of sap. Check valves kept tapholes from healing too quickly without harming trees or adversely affecting the syrup.

· · · · · · · ·

"TAKE CARE OF the trees and they will take care of you," is Rick Marsh's mantra. A fireplug of a man with straight gray hair and a bushy mustache, he's not completely sold on check valves. A former president of the North American Maple Syrup Council, for many years he ran Vermont Maple Outlet, a long, low salesroom and gift shop on busy State Route 15 in Jeffersonville. It includes a small museum with knotty-pine walls and an oil-fired demonstration evaporator. The east end of the building contains his packing room and candy-making area. Today, his daughter and son-in-law run the retail business. He still sugars and is a sales manager for CDL USA, a Canadian-headquartered maple equipment manufacturer that competes with Leader.

Rick's family has been on the land since 1909, and like so many sugaring operations, his was a dairy farm before going maple full time. Around the turn of the twenty-first century he built a new sugarhouse on the site of one dating to 1840. Sided with T-111 plywood, it's set back from the road and built into a hillside.

Though he remembers fondly the camaraderie of collecting from buckets when he and his companions told jokes and had snowball fights years ago, he likes better that technology has enabled his eleven thousand taps to outproduce what he used to get from twenty-one thousand. He also buys sap from several thousand taps belonging to someone else. Better tubing, vacuum, and RO are key, he said.

Despite manufacturer claims and the accolades of many sugarmakers, Rick is not so keen on check valves. He tried twelve hundred of them shortly after they came out and found that they quit producing earlier than many of his other taps. They're not so critical if you have reliable vacuum, he told me. They might benefit early tappers in places that get January runs, but in his northern Vermont location their effect, he claims, isn't so dramatic. If you keep tubing clean and replace it regularly, check valves are not such a big deal. He favors the "smart spout" sold by CDL, the company he represents. Made of a soft, white plastic, it forms a better seal at the taphole, Rick says, making vacuum more effective and thereby reducing the possibility of bacteria developing. The soft plastic is also less likely to damage trees than harder materials that can act like a wedge.

As he extolled the smart spout's virtues, I remembered rumbles of concern from some sugarmakers about the public-private partnership between Leader and the Proctor Center. They worried that the center might be chasing industry research dollars and patent money. "It's not good for the industry if research goes too commercial," one producer told me.

While maple people are typically generous with their knowledge, many had strong loyalties to particular brands of equipment, not unlike the way many people feel about cars. Such allegiances could stir vigorous debate. Even something as seemingly simple and inexpensive as a spout had an astounding number of patented variations that accrued partisans. Star Line had its "Intelligent Thin Walled" spouts. H2O Innovation had something called "ERAtube" spouts, and the Lapierre company touted its "Zero-Micro-Leaks" spout. Other companies have their own variations, and all are eager to develop the next essential innovation.

Rick and I stood in sunlight by the sugarhouse door on an unusually warm April day, Mount Mansfield's still leafless slopes visible in the distance. I thought of the Proctor Center nestled in woods on the other side.

. . . .

J. MARK HARRAN is an athletic-looking man in his seventies, with large glasses that magnify gray-blue eyes. President of the Connecticut Maple Syrup Producers Association, he is an eager evangelist for maple. His own operation, in Litchfield, is "one thousand taps and growing." His sugarhouse, a hundred-year-old converted garage, features a two-by-six oil-fired evaporator with a Steam-Away and a computerized probe to measure liquid depth in the pan. The rig has a showroom shine.

With its nearby and affluent market, Connecticut's industry has the potential for phenomenal growth, according to Mark. "Our producers satisfy only 5 to 10 percent of the state's syrup consumption," he said. He wants native syrup on supermarket shelves and on pallets in big-box stores. He's urging sugarmakers to get Universal Product Code (UPC) labels for their syrup, a necessity for large retailers. He sees possibilities with overseas exports. Only one-tenth of 1 percent of tappable trees are in production, he lamented, but then grew excited over future prospects.

Mark was a senior vice president for marketing and sales at General Foods. While he was there, the last real maple was taken out of the Log Cabin Syrup formula because it was expensive and technology enabled the company to produce a somewhat similar flavor with corn syrup. He smiled. "I'm now doing penance," he said.

Mark brimmed with maple facts, figures, and anecdotes that spilled out of him like sap from a tap on a sunny day in the high forties. He delighted in telling stories, like the one about the time he left an evaporator valve open and found hot syrup puddling on his shoes. He wants Connecticut syrup competing on the world stage and fretted that a local congressman on a European trade mission saw Canadian syrup "displayed everywhere." Recent studies, he said, show maple syrup has "the lowest calories and highest nutrition of any sweetener."

At an age when many people wax nostalgic and revel in past glories, Mark enthuses over the future of maple syrup in this compact state of mostly small producers. He installed RO a couple of years ago. He's using check valves, and most of his taps are on vacuum, each of which doubles the amount of sap he gets per tap. On a chilly Washington's birthday, we walked a sloping hayfield and looked at a miniature pump housed in a tiny plywood shed. Scaling down the size and cost of technology for small producers is critical to the survival of widespread maple syrup production in a place like Connecticut, which, because of market proximity, commands by far the highest price per gallon of syrup—seventy-one dollars in 2013. He's bullish on check-valve taps because they are cheap and particularly useful here where the season often starts a month earlier than it did less than a generation ago.

Mark effervesces about RO, which is increasingly more compact and less expensive. It's "revolutionary," he said. The machine he bought for about $8,500 would have sold for $20,000 about a decade ago. Even bringing the sap up to 8 percent sugar reduces one thousand gallons to about two hundred and cuts boiling time fourfold. He's saving about $3,000 a year in oil, and his electricity bill has increased only moderately since plugging in the RO. At the same time, "we've cut air emissions dramatically," he said proudly.

Like many successful sugarmakers, Mark knows how to ride the wave of change. He has a "beauty bucket" on display near his sugarhouse, but he mostly uses tubing. He has great old-time maple memories from childhood and is steeped in sugar-making lore, but he also finds romance and excitement in the challenges and opportunities of technology. Regardless of his age, in his marketing savvy and equal grasp of both innovation and heritage Mark may be the very model of a modern maple sugarmaker. As Burr Morse so succinctly put it, "changes are insuring the future of our industry."

There's no telling how far innovation will go or where it will end. Dr. Perkins and colleagues recently experimented with cutting maple saplings off at waist height, covering the cuts with tightly sealed plastic bags, and pumping sap out of the stumps and into tubing under high vacuum. Could plantations of saplings replace tapping wild trees? With a traditional sugarbush providing forty gallons of syrup per acre from about eighty mature trees, and the new method producing perhaps four hundred gallons from six thousand saplings, possibilities beckon. Still, much work needs to be done. Despite experimental results, there's no conclusive evidence that this can be done economically and sustainably, and some highly knowledgeable people in the field feel it is impossible.

Maple Pecan Pie

Yield: 6–8 servings

INGREDIENTS

3 eggs
1 cup firmly packed brown sugar
¼ cup granulated sugar
½ teaspoon salt
2 tablespoons all-purpose flour
1 cup maple syrup
3 tablespoons unsalted butter, melted
1½ cups pecans
1 unbaked 9-inch pie shell

DIRECTIONS

1. Preheat the oven to 400°F.
2. In a medium bowl, combine the eggs, sugars, salt, flour,
   Connecticut maple syrup, and butter.
3. Stir in the pecans.
4. Pour into the pie shell.
5. Bake for 45 minutes, or until set.

Recipe by Kay Carroll

Maple Walnut Oat Scones

Yield: 16 scones

INGREDIENTS

1½ cups flour
1 cup quick rolled oats
2 tablespoons sugar
3½ teaspoons baking powder
½ teaspoon salt
½ teaspoon cinnamon
½ cup (1 stick) butter or margarine
½ to ⅔ cup milk
3 tablespoons chopped walnuts
¼ cup pure maple syrup

DIRECTIONS

1. Heat the oven to 425°F.
2. Combine the flour, quick oats, sugar, baking power, salt, and cinnamon.
3. Cut in the butter with a pastry blender until mixture is crumbly.
4. Add milk, walnuts, and maple syrup just until dry ingredients are moist.
5. On a floured surface, gently knead dough five to six times.
6. Form into a ball and divide dough in half. Press each half into a 6-to-7-inch circle.
7. Cut dough into eight wedges and repeat with second half of the dough.
8. Place the dough wedges onto a nonstick cookie sheet.
9. Bake at 425° for 10–12 minutes.

You can also divide the dough into three rounds for smaller scones. Cut into twenty-four wedges. Adjust the baking time by 1–2 minutes.

Recipe by Carolyn Gimbrone and Susan Derby

The Miracle of Maples

NOT SINCE DRUID DAYS, perhaps, have trees been so revered by an organized group as maples are by sugarmakers. "Sugar maples are the most significant tree in the world for what they give to human-kind," J. Mark Harran has told me with an earnestness usually reserved for statements of religious faith. It was a cold, late-February day, and sap hadn't run for a week. Mark was pensive. We walked past his stately 1786 center-chimney home and entered the knotty-pine sugarhouse with its gleaming stainless evaporator tossing light into the room like a mirror. Surrounded by all the tools of sugar making, he was as eager as a kid waiting for a snowfall to cancel school.

"There's no properly planted New England village without its sugar maples," wrote naturalist Donald Culross Peattie in a 1950 book about trees. "On a street where great maples arch, letting down their shining benediction, people seem to walk as if they had already gone to glory." Harran's Litchfield, Connecticut, its spacious green dotted with historic monuments and surrounded by dignified classic buildings that recall an earlier era, is just such a village.

No doubt calling on talents that made him a successful food company marketing executive, the angular Harran recited the maple's virtues like a cheerleader urging his team to victory. "Besides syrup," he said, "it provides the only three-color autumn foliage, shade, flooring, furniture, and a high Btu value." Fascinated with the tree's every aspect, he terms its sap sugar content "a miracle." Briefly lifting heavy plastic-frame glasses from his face, he squinted into the distance as if looking for something far off. "Earth has provided," he remarked in a soft, measured tone, "and the sugar maple is on the high-order side."

· · · · · · ·

OF THE 148 maple species (genus *Acer*) found in the Northern Hemisphere, thirteen are native to North America, and all are tappable to some extent. Among those commonly found in New England, red maple (*Acer rubrum*), also nicknamed swamp maple, and silver maple (*Acer saccharinum*), sometimes called white or river maple, both can yield syrup, though their sap is less sweet than that of the aptly named sugar maple (*Acer saccharum*), which typically registers at between 2.5 percent sugar. Frequently found in more-developed areas, Norway maple (*Acer platanoides*) can be tapped, though it's often derided as an invasive species. Growing mostly in the Midwest, black maple (*Acer nigrum*) is the only species with sap as sweet as sugar maple. It was long thought of as a sugar maple subspecies, and distinguishing between the two is largely an academic exercise.

Often with half the sweetness of sugar maple, red and silver maple have been pejoratively called the "the poor man's" syrup trees, and traditionally the amount of fuel needed to produce a sufficiently sugary product has made tapping them prohibitively expensive. With the ability to concentrate sugar quickly and cheaply by using RO, the paradigm has changed, though these trees' earlier budding tendency potentially makes for a shorter sap-collection season. Norway maple is typically planted in new developments because it grows fast and thrives in poor and compacted soils. It's also reviled and even banned in some places because its highly aggressive growth habit, profligate seed production, and dense shade outcompete native species once it becomes naturalized in suburban and urban areas. Despite having a previous "strong aversion" to the tree, Mike Farrell has tasted Norway maple syrup and found it "quite delicious."

It's fortunate that new technology enables sugarmakers to use less-sweet maples, especially red maple, which is increasingly common and may soon be the dominant tree in much of the Northeast. Regardless, only sugar maples inspire awe, reverence even. "Walking in my sugar grove is like going to church," Shelburne, Massachusetts, sugarmaker Jerry Dubie told me. It's a sentiment many syrup producers express when they think of hushed woodlands filled with tall sugar maples where light slants down as if from clerestory windows. Mike Girard likens his trees to children. He's concerned for their welfare, wants to know how they're doing.

• • • • • • •

WHILE SUGARMAKERS might get a bit misty about their trees, you'd expect less romance from a veteran forest ecologist who has spent decades studying minute sylvan phenomena and taking tedious measurements for complex calculations. Dr. Charles Canham has studied many species but has a special affection for sugar maple.

He has spent a lot of time examining the architecture of trees. In its elegant regularity and symmetry, sugar maple seems to him an almost ideal form. It's an emotional response, admits the soft-spoken scientist, which harks back to his younger days when he wandered woodlands near Storm King Mountain on the Hudson River. It was the 1970s, at the height of controversy over a pump storage facility whose defeat was an environmental-law landmark. Walking the rugged oaky ground on the mountain's slopes, Charlie entered a grove of sugar maples with their deeper, greener shade, uniform canopy, and richer, spongier soils. He was struck by the peacefulness of the scene, disturbed only by surveyor's stakes that marked its potential destruction. The beauty and tranquility of that moment, coupled with the threat that it could quickly be lost forever, never left him.

• • • • • • •

THE SUGAR MAPLE belt cuts a wide swath across the eastern part of the continent. Its northern boundary stretches from the mouth of the St. Lawrence River in Canada to southeastern Manitoba, south to northern Georgia, and west to the left border of Minnesota, central Iowa, eastern Kansas, and Missouri. In favorable sites with moist, deep soil, it can be found as far south as Texas and Louisiana. Elevation plays a role, and in the northern reaches sugar maple grows at up to twenty-five hundred feet, while in southern areas it can thrive at heights of three thousand to fifty-five hundred feet.

Mature sugar maples range from seventy to ninety feet tall and achieve breast-height diameters (at four and a half feet above the ground) of two to three feet. Under optimal conditions, specimens one hundred feet tall are possible. The largest was a behemoth from West Virginia that grew 110 feet tall and five and a half feet in diameter, according to Cornell University. Growing in open fields, sugar maples assume an oval shape and branch near the ground. In the woods they are more columnar, with a tufted crown stretching to the canopy. A resilient tree, it survives high winds, fierce cold, and repeated deer browsing. Its stump sprouts when cut. Seedlings can wait patiently through decades of dense shade until a natural or human disturbance provides sunshine and an opportunity to quickly rise to maturity.

Sugar maple's brilliant tricolored fall leaves—orange, red, yellow—and handsome elliptical shape make it a popular ornamental planting in parks, residential yards, and at institutions. As a street tree, its desirability has waned somewhat because of sensitivity to root compaction and pollution, especially road salt. Despite such susceptibility, the tree often exhibits a capacity to withstand changing conditions. I remember a national champion, gnarly and unevenly branched, that survived many years at the edge of a commuter parking lot in Norwich, Connecticut, where it grew ninety-one feet tall with a trunk circumference of twenty-three feet. The last marker of what had once been a field, the tree succumbed about a generation ago.

In good conditions, sugar maples grow roughly a foot and gain two-tenths of an inch in girth per year for the first three or four decades. They reach tapping size of ten to twelve inches in diameter after thirty-five to sixty years. In about 140 to 150 years they grow no taller, and radial growth slows dramatically. Although uncommon, ancient stands can range from three hundred to four hundred years old.

Stately, almost regal in their maturity, sugar maples are attractive year-round. Not long after the last drop of sap is collected and the taps pulled, they become covered with lacy, pendant green flowers that suffuse the landscape with yellowish haze. They are pollinated by bees, and at times provide some of the year's first nectar. At leaf-out they slowly open like little shriveled hands until their distinctive five-lobed shape, wider than long, reaches full span at three to six inches. Deep green above and paler below, they provide dense shade through the most blistering summer. Come September, the inch to inch-and-a-half paired winged fruit known as samaras, or keys, hang thick on the branches, dropping in helicopter whirls to the delight of children of all ages who separate the pieces, peel open the ends, and paste them on their noses.

The Bolduc brothers with an old friend

Flaming fall color has probably been the maple's greatest attraction and economic value ever since tourism's rise in the late nineteenth century. Garnering such attention is good for syrup producers, who can sell the tree's sweet essence to tourists eager to take home a memory of the gaudy display. But for sugarmakers, perhaps it's the leafless, skeletal winter image presaging sapping season that carries the most allure. Especially beautiful are open-field trees with their thick network of ascending branches above a stout trunk rising to a symmetrical oval crown. It's then that the bark, evolving like a human face with age, is most evident. At first smooth and dark gray, as they age trees develop rough vertical ridges and grooves, which become long picturesque plates that peel away from the trunk on mature trees.

While questions of an afterlife for humans are filled with controversy, maples harvested for their wood can become generation-lasting products with beauty that will command the respect even of those who don't know the difference between cane and maple sugar. Valued for being hard, close-grained, and durable, maple wood is used in flooring, furniture, bowling alleys and pins, musical instruments, bas-

ketball courts and dance floors, wooden spoons and rolling pins, as
well as baseball bats. It's particularly valuable and attractive when the
grain is distorted, creating tiger, flame, or bird's-eye patterns. Spalted
wood—irregularly discolored by fungi—is much sought after for
bowls and other decorative objects. Dotted and streaked from years
of sugaring, taphole lumber is becoming increasingly popular for decorative uses.

Historically, maple wood played an even more important role for
gunstocks, ship interiors, butter molds, spinning wheels, and carriage-
wheel spokes. In the early industrial era, textile shuttles and spools
were of maple, as was wooden type for printing. For its compact, long-
lasting energy value as firewood, maple has always been esteemed by
those who heat with wood or simply enjoy the warmth and ceremony
of a fire.

• • • • • • •

STEVE BRODERICK is a sugarmaker who knows trees and how to
explain their wonders to landowners and the public at large. A lanky,
bearded, and bespectacled man with pale blue eyes and a quiet, sym-
pathetic voice, he spent thirty years as a forester and educator with
the University of Connecticut cooperative extension. When Steve
talks trees, people listen. He has marked woods for thinning, ad-
vised landowners on timber stand improvement, and taught classes
on land-use regulation, forest management, and a popular intro-
ductory course on maple sugaring. His first experience of sugaring
was as a toddler on his great-uncle Harold's Wilmington, Vermont,
dairy farm, and as a young man he tapped the ancient maples on the
Brooklyn, Connecticut, town green, boiling outside with sap from
up to thirty trees. Later he fabricated a homemade evaporator from
a 275-gallon oil tank perched on its side and cut on top to fit a pan
made from a folded sheet of stainless steel. Living at the time in a
town where a lot of Finns had settled early in the twentieth century,
he placed the contraption in an old sauna building from which he had
knocked out the louvers.

"I like the social aspect of sugaring," he told me from the spacious
sugarhouse with a poured concrete floor that he built with a friend.

"The first selectman stopped by a few nights ago for a chat and a beer." His fair face grew ruddy with heat as he opened the door on the arch and tossed a few chunks of wood into the fire. Of course, a forester's first love is trees, and the best part of sugaring, he admitted, is that "it gets me outdoors into the woods at a time of year when I'd normally be inside. When sugaring's done, I guess it's time to go fishing," he added with a wink.

While farmers, as a group, are most likely to be sugarmakers, no single profession comes to maple sugaring with as much enthusiasm as those foresters who would rather tap than cut down a maple. It's a natural fit for those who care for and know something about trees. Steve's sugarbush is stocked with well-spaced oak, maple, and some pine, threaded by ancient stone walls, and divided by well-planned paths where pools of dappled sunlight reach the leafy floor. After a quarter century of thinning and careful management, it was like a series of carefully arranged rooms. Walking with him was a revelation.

Steve not only knew the species of each leafless tree on that blustery January day; he knew them as individuals by how fast they had grown, their tropisms from struggling for sun, their cracked bark and burls caused by insect damage, and how they responded to drought and rain, frigid days, and searing heat. He looked at the tightness of bark, the shape of crowns. By topography and location of timber, both living and dead, he could point out the direction of windstorms decades past; he knew where lightning had struck, and could trace successive logging operations by stumps and basal damage. He saw patterns and structure where I just saw forest. He didn't need X-ray vision to see things invisible to me. Looking at a tree, he could imagine its vascular system as I might a road map. He had a relationship with this place.

At a glance able to judge soil fertility and moisture, exposure to wind and hours of available sunlight, the trained eye of a forester looks at trees differently than most sugarmakers, he told me. Steve sees the woods not just as they are or might be in a year or two, but how they will be over the decades. Sugaring was not just about syrup; it was about managing a living community of complex interactions. Though a well-managed sugarbush will yield more and sweeter sap, many sugarmakers are reluctant to trim trees. They fear it will create havoc with tubing. Most of all, cutting a ten- or twelve-inch maple, even when crowded, is considered by some a kind of cardinal sin.

The camaraderie Steve enjoys in the sugarhouse extends to the woods, where he can read the body language of the landscape and hear the stories the trees tell about their struggle for light, water, and soil. He seemed to hear the large old-timers, so-called wolf trees that had grown up when his sugarbush was an open field, arguing with the pole timber as they angled for space. He sensed the longing of mature trees throwing seeds to the wind and seeking a sweet spot of moist dark soil among the stones and bedrock. There was effervescence in his voice, a lighter step as we made our way through the woods, and despite the hard-nosed scientist bred by years of training, he looked at the trees with empathy, had almost a sixth sense about them. "I walk this land every day and never tire of it," he told me as he gestured to the trees around us. "I try to notice at least one new thing every time, the growth of a plant, a fallen branch."

· · · · · · ·

DURING THE growing season, maples are grand solar collectors, each leaf absorbing sunshine to create food. A tappable forest tree about fifteen inches in diameter and fifty feet tall probably has over 156,000 leaves, or about eighty-five hundred square feet of photosynthesizing power. For a twenty-inch-diameter specimen, the numbers jump to almost 302,000 leaves covering sixteen thousand square feet, according to a rough back-of-the-envelope calculation made by Charles Canham. Open-field individuals have much larger crowns with much greater leaf coverage.

In an alchemy of absorbed water, carbon dioxide, and sun, photosynthesis is a process that gathers energy from sunlight and uses it to turn water and carbon dioxide into carbohydrates or sugars that sustain the tree while growing. Some of this food is stored, mostly as starch, to keep the tree alive during the cold, leafless months and to jump start growth in spring. As winter progresses, some starch is reconverted to sucrose. The sugar content of sap can vary depending on a tree's health, genetics, site conditions, the size of the crown, and weather during the previous growing season. Sweetness of sap is much lower in fall, and in spring it rises to a crescendo before tailing off as buds start to break.

It is common knowledge that sap flows with the seesaw fluctuations of temperature above and below the freezing mark. But while scientists have been studying maple hydraulics since the nineteenth century, and much has been learned in the past few decades, the process is not entirely understood. Despite "dozens of papers written on how and why sap flows," Michael Farrell writes, "it still remains somewhat of a mystery." Back in the 1950s, the Nearings counted a dozen theories of sap flow: "peristaltic action, osmosis, capillarity, atmospheric pressure, cohesive power of water, adsorption, transpiration, root pressure, gas pressure, chemical ferments, electrical attraction, local action of living cells." Though today we know that sap flow is based on pressure differential in the tree, what seems like a simple explanation is full of complexity.

Most of a living tree is not alive. Strangely called heartwood, this dead component gives trees their strength and structure and is the part we are familiar with in everything from house framing to pencils. Just below the rough, crusty bark there is life in a thin layer called cambium, where the tree's vascular system lies. The plumbing is not in the form of long pipes, but rather a network of slender, vertically oriented cells connected to one another. Water is conducted through this system of vessels called xylem, while sugars produced via photosynthesis move down the leaves through a network of tubes called phloem. Each year new xylem and phloem layers are added, while some of the older layers dry out and become heartwood.

Negative pressure (suction) builds in a maple's plumbing when temperatures fall below freezing, while positive pressure results when temperatures rise. Fiber cells in the xylem surrounding sap-conducting vessels are, unlike in most trees, filled with air rather than liquid. With freezing, ice crystals form within the fiber cells somewhat like frost on a windshield, causing a drop in humidity within those fiber cells and generating a rush of moisture from adjacent liquid-containing vessels. The additional moisture causes the ice crystals to grow, compressing the air and resulting in more sap movement into the fiber cells. This strong suction, augmented by contracting and dissolving air bubbles in the cooling sap, draws water from the roots when the ground isn't frozen and continues until all the tree's sap ices up.

When temperatures soar above freezing again and branches thaw, the pressure goes quickly from negative to positive because thawing ice in the fiber cells enables bubbles to expand and forces sap back into the liquid-transmitting vessels. At the same time, gravity exerts downward pressure from thawing ice in the branches, and sucrose in thawed sap draws water out of the fibers and into the vessels by osmosis. Combined, these phenomena can exert as much as forty pounds of pressure per square inch near the base of the trunk and cause sap to drip out through a tap or wound, such as a broken branch. When temperatures stop fluctuating, pressure dissipates and sap stops flowing, unless a tap is on vacuum.

• • • • • • • •

ON A FRIGID January morning, I joined sugarmaker and Connecticut Department of Energy and Environmental Protection forester Jerry Milne at a commuter parking lot. After a few turns, he drove along narrow and twisty Echo Valley Road in Newtown and parked his state pickup just off the pavement in Paugussett State Forest. Temperatures were in the single digits, there was little wind, and sap in the trees was locked up tight.

Connecticut has over thirty state forests, with of total of over 175,000 acres, and I've spent many days in them hiking, hunting, botanizing, fishing, picnicking, and wildlife watching, but this spot was unlike any other I'd visited. Before us was an almost perfect sugar grove of about six acres containing well-spaced maples strung together by a network of blue tubing glowing almost iridescently in sunlit woods covered with a deep quilt of reflective snow. The land faced east and rolled gradually down to frozen Lake Lillinonah, beyond which was a haystack-like hill.

"It may be the sweetest woods in Connecticut," Jerry said. He has actively managed the property for years as a demonstration sugarbush where landowners and the general public can learn best silvicultural practices for promoting maple growth. Jerry is an enthusiast, and there was a lilt to his voice as he told me how the grove got started about 1960 when large sugar maples along a bordering stone wall scattered seeds in what was abandoned pasture. Thousands of tiny seedlings carpeted the ground, competing for sunlight, until by the 1980s there were a few hundred trees per acre growing slowly, with trunks averaging six inches in diameter. With the trees still fairly small, "it presented an ideal time to create a sugarbush of well-spaced, high-quality, productive trees," he observed with quiet professionalism. But then his eyes widened and excitement came into his voice. "I mean, what could be better than a topographical aspect to capture the morning sun along with moist, well-drained, and loamy Charlton soil, the most fertile in the state."

Jerry handed me a tree caliper for measuring the diameter of trunks, and he picked up a tablet device for recording data as we trudged through the snow, taking inventory while he related the history of this wondrous grove. First, he said, the tallest maples with the largest crowns were identified as potential crop trees and further selected for trunks with the fewest defects and forks. Chosen trees were at least twenty-five to thirty feet apart. Next, the sugar content of the sap was measured and compared. Sweeter, better-formed trees were selected for the sugarbush, and competing ones were sold for firewood, especially those whose crowns touched the crop trees. After several years of thinning, Jerry found the remaining trees had doubled their growth rate. In little more than a decade and a half, many of the original seedlings had reached a twelve-inch diameter and were ready to tap.

Jerry is a tall and long-legged man with a thick, dark beard. He's not just comfortable among the trees; he seems *of* the woods. Where I struggled to walk in the deep snow, he seemed to move effortlessly, taking down numbers as I measured trunks at breast height. He caught the sugaring bug in forestry school and started with thirty taps and a barrel evaporator with a flat pan. Though he now boils on a two-by-four rig, he has stayed small because he doesn't want sugaring to become work. He taps roadside and backyard trees and those on his town green. Syrup is given away to friends and neighbors, and he enters a sample in a nearby agricultural fair. Though some foresters and sugarmakers look at trees as a commodity, Jerry's passion for maples transcends commercialism. "The sugar orchard is a living, growing organism," he told me. "You can't damage the bark with machines or run over roots and not have consequences."

When the trees became big enough to tap, they were leased to a commercial syrup producer. Fifty taps was the limit the first year, but it didn't take many seasons for there to be four hundred. Now there are over six hundred. "The syrup makers used to squeal pretty loud when I'd mark a sugar maple for culling," Jerry admitted with a grin, "but they've seen the results in a healthier stand and more sap."

As if on cue, the stocky and stubble-cheeked Berecz bothers from Woodbury Sugarshed showed up to scout more taps and lay out tubing. Though quiet at first, as soon as we got past pleasantries and started talking maple they became loquacious. Walking the uneven, sloping ground with maps and a surveyor's rod and transit, they worked their way slowly through a newly opened part of the grove, figuring slope, tap numbers, and tank locations. The site of a pump was carefully discussed. More thinning was also on their mind, with some birch, hickory, and big tulip trees needing cutting. As Jerry predicted, they shuddered when he suggested a few maples should come out.

Paugussett was the first state forest with a demonstration sugarbush, but now there are several. With timber harvests commanding more money, Jerry admitted, it doesn't pay for the state to maintain sugarbushes just for the small lease income and fifty cents per tap. But it's a different way of looking at the value of trees where a long straight trunk is not as important as a big crown, and fewer stems per acre are acceptable. The public experiences a different kind of managed forest, he said. He looked around us as the Berecz brothers moved toward the lake. Under a deep and cloudless azure sky, the gray trunks seemed to radiate an internal light. "Trees look dead to most folks in winter," he said, his dark eyes widening, "but something important is going on. Sugarmakers and foresters see a stirring beneath the bark that is invisible to average people."

A forestry school class with a tree-improvement project that involved him in breeding sugar maples for higher sugar content sparked

Jerry's interest in syrup making. Ever since, he's been obsessed with sweet trees. Noting that it takes forty-three gallons of 2 percent sap compared to twenty-four and a half gallons of 3.5 percent sap to make a gallon of syrup, Jerry has rigorously tested the Paugussett trees and done all he can to encourage the sweet ones. If a tree could yield 10 percent sap, only eight and six-tenths gallons would be required, an amazing difference.

· · · · · · · ·

TEN PERCENT TREES are a kind of holy grail. Generally, large specimens with spreading crowns in open areas produce the sweetest sap, but the extent to which this was a function of the environment or a characteristic that could be passed from parent to progeny was for many years an open question.

When sugaring was at its nadir before widespread use of tubing or the advent of RO, genetic improvement of trees for sap sugar and volume seemed a good way of reducing labor and fuel costs. In the 1950s, the Proctor Center's Fred Taylor found that individual trees and stands could differ in sap sweetness by as much as 100 percent. A more extensive survey of over twenty-one thousand trees published in the early 1970s found sap ranging from 0.7 to 10.8 percent sugar and raised the question of whether such differences were genetically determined. Scientists became busy with selective breeding projects in several states, including Vermont, New York, and Ohio.

Cornell University probably has the longest ongoing project to produce supersweet maples. Of the twenty-one thousand originally tested trees, fifty-three were selected for their genetic potential to produce sweet sap. Some trees were cloned, with cuttings grafted onto the rootstock. Other cuttings were rooted by treating them with hormones in a greenhouse using strict regimes of temperature, light, and nutrients. It was tedious, almost heroic work that took years.

Cuttings grafted onto rootstock were planted at a U.S. Forest Service site in Grand Isle, Vermont, and later a second group was planted at Cornell's Uihlein Sugar Maple Field Station in Lake Placid, New York, forming two clonal banks. Using trees grown from seeds harvested from the clonal banks, progeny tests were conducted in two locations where seeds were planted at relatively uniform sites. Seven years later, the trees were tested for sweetness, and a partial genetic connection was found. The best trees from these progeny were planted in a university orchard to produce seeds for growers.

Trees descended from these experimental plantings are sold today by a few growers, including Forest Keeling Nursery in Elsberry, Missouri, which propagates them via a patented multistep system of containers emphasizing root production. Sold in two-gallon pots for just under fifteen dollars (a few dollars more than regular sugar maples), they range from eighteen inches to three feet tall. Sugarmakers are the principal purchasers of these 30 percent sweeter trees, according to company president Wayne Lovelace. Demand is strong, and when I contacted them early in 2014 the plants were out of stock.

Despite a couple of decades of excitement and furious scientific work, the gold rush to produce sweet trees is largely over. All the researchers working on the program at Cornell have retired. The Proctor Center has a plantation established in 1960, but it's no longer regularly maintained, Dr. Perkins told me. Programs remain elsewhere, but with the development of vacuum, volumes of sap from ordinary trees have vastly improved, while ro has made them functionally supersweet. Furthermore, there is a long wait before extra-sweet seedlings are tappable, some concern for genetic diversity if there is widespread planting of trees derived from only fifty-three parents, and the possibility that seeds from high-sugar trees will be fertilized by those with normal sugar content.

Nevertheless, Farrell observes, sugarmakers with 30 percent sweeter trees will produce more syrup more quickly, whether they have ro or not. He sees increasing interest in planting sweet trees around homes and sugarhouses as a legacy for the sugarmaker's children and grandchildren. Mike Girard planted some Cornell supersweets on his front lawn in Heath, Massachusetts. He likes tree planting, and his place has been a certified tree farm since 1977. Of the roughly 350 maples he has planted over the past thirty years, about 250 have survived. Planting them seems to matter more to him than the possibility he'll harvest sap someday. During a conversation in his sugarhouse, he leaned back with thumbs in the front pockets of his jeans. "The sweeter the tree, the slower it grows, is the old saying." He smiled. "Actually, I'm not sure it's true."

. . . .

DESPITE ALL THE science about tree physiology, sap flow, and weather forecasting, predicting a sap run remains a crapshoot. No wonder there are so many pithy old-time maxims about maple weather. The Nearings collected some of these puzzling and often inconsistent sayings, all of which combine truth with exaggeration and contradiction. These are some of my favorites:

- Sap runs better by day than by night.
- Sixty-three percent of the sap is said to drop before noon.
- The darker the evening, the sooner sap will stop.
- The nearer the occurrence of a freeze or snowstorm that sap is caught, the sweeter it is.
- The more intense the cold, the greater the quantity of sugar in the sap.
- During clear weather more sap is produced than during cloudy weather.

Regardless of whether he was right or not, perhaps Burr Morse has said it best: "Good weather is bad for sugarmakers and bad weather is good."

Sometimes there are seemingly perfect conditions, like a night in the mid-twenties followed by a bright sunny day in the mid-forties when sap should, theoretically, be pouring from tapholes, but there is barely a trickle. Other days might be overcast and in the high thirties, but sap pulses like a heartbeat and buckets can overflow. Of course, tree size, location, the cleanliness of tapholes, the time of the season, soil moisture, and atmospheric pressure are among the imponderable variables. At times, it just seems that the trees have a will of their own. As a result, sugarmakers are loath to make predictions. "Whenever we think we know what kind of sap flow to expect, Mother Nature usually throws us a curveball that can make us look foolish," Farrell writes.

Call it contrariness, independence, or indomitable flux, the often unpredictable flow of sap gives the trees personality. Add that to the graceful artistry with which they adorn our landscape year-round and the host of useful products they supply, and it's no wonder Anna Botsford Comstock could write that "the sugar maple, combining beauty with many kinds of utility, is dear to the American heart."

Baked Apples

Yield: 4 baked apples

INGREDIENTS
4 large, firm, tart apples
⅓ cup packed brown sugar
¼ cup raisins
2 teaspoons cinnamon
⅛ teaspoon nutmeg
⅓ cup low-fat yogurt
¼ cup maple syrup

DIRECTIONS
1. Heat the oven to 375°F.
2. Core the apples and remove one inch of skin around the center of each apple to prevent the skin from splitting.
3. Place the apples upright in baking dish.
4. In a small bowl, combine the brown sugar, raisins, cinnamon, and nutmeg. Spoon this into the center of each apple.
5. Pour water, about ¼-inch deep, into the baking dish around the apples. This will help them steam and cook.
6. Bake uncovered about 30−40 minutes or until apples are tender when pierced with a fork. Take care when removing them from the baking dish, as the baked apples stay very hot.
7. Combine the yogurt and maple syrup to make the sauce to pour over the baked apples just before serving.

Maple-Coated Nuts

Yield: 3 cups

INGREDIENTS

3 cups unsalted nuts
½ cup maple syrup
¼ cup water

DIRECTIONS

1. Combine the nuts, maple syrup, and water in a heavy pan.
2. Over medium-low heat, bring the mixture to a simmer, stirring constantly, until the nuts absorb the maple syrup.
3. If you are not planning to eat them right away, spread the maple-coated nuts on a lightly buttered cookie sheet and bake them at 325°F for about 10 minutes or until dry. Keep a close watch on the nuts and carefully stir them a few times during the baking to prevent burning.
4. When cool, store in a tightly covered container.

One Taste and You're
in the Snowy Woods

ON A WARM, sunny afternoon a few days past Lincoln's birthday some years ago I was drilling a taphole in a large maple that stood at the corner of Main and Center Streets about a block from my home in Collinsville. Corkscrews of fresh, light heartwood rode their way along the bit and dropped to the ground. With a soft squeal of brakes, a vintage Chevy Impala pulled over and a middle-aged man with thinning red hair rolled down the window. "Hey, there! Whatcha doin'?" he asked. With a galvanized bucket beside me, I thought the answer obvious. However, being in the business of selling syrup, I didn't want to lose an opportunity. I replied with polite enthusiasm so as not to make the driver feel stupid. "Oh," he said, somewhat surprised, "I thought that only happened in Vermont." Momentarily I was speechless, struck dumb by the absurdity. The car pulled away with a roar before I could muster a reply. I shook my head and returned to my business, drilling holes and hanging buckets, over seventy that day, happy to hear the ping of drops against the battered old metal.

Of course, syrup can be made wherever the right maples experience freeze-and-thaw cycles. It's produced commercially in at least part of nearly twenty states and four Canadian provinces. Nevertheless, there may be no place so much associated with a particular agricultural commodity and its mythic lifestyle as Vermont and maple syrup. The two are more intimately bound than Florida and oranges, Maine and lobster, Idaho and potatoes, Iowa and corn. Say "Vermont" in a kind of verbal Rorschach test and the first thing that comes to mind is maple syrup. By law, maple was declared the official flavor of the state in 1993, and the Vermont state quarter bears an image of sugar maples with sap buckets.

It's not just the sweet stuff that people think of, for maple syrup is evocative of a way of life, an image reinforced every time some of the golden liquid is poured from typical containers bearing nostalgic rural scenes. Usually there's snow on the ground, an old-timey sugarhouse, a stack of firewood, a stone wall, and stately trees bearing buckets. Sometimes there's a team of horses pulling a sled with a gathering tank, a means of collecting sap that hasn't been widely used for generations. I've never seen a label showing so much as a foot of tubing or the big pump trucks major producers use to collect sap.

Most syrup labels reinforce Vermont's popular image—rural simplicity, a clean environment, and honest labor. Indeed, although it has only about a fifth of Quebec's annual production, Vermont is by far the leading U.S. producing state, with almost 4.3 million taps and over 1.3 million gallons of syrup, representing about 42 percent of U.S. production. But the connection between the Green Mountain State and syrup is not just a matter of gallons or taps, nor is it an accident. It's the result of shrewd Yankee marketing that began with formation of the Vermont Maple Sugar Makers Association (VMSMA) in 1893. The organization has worked tirelessly to bolster the notion of syrup as a reservoir of traditional American values and establish a narrative of a genuine, natural, and pure product valued not only for its distinctive taste but also its cultural significance.

Considered by some the first agricultural organization in the country devoted to a single commodity, the VMSMA was formed "to improve quality, increase the quantity and protect manufacturers and consumers from the many fraudulent preparations placed on the market as pure maple goods." Within a year, the association had prepared a pamphlet and label for the use of its members that would set the tone for future efforts. The pamphlet depicts an old-fashioned image of a man at the forest's edge sitting atop a woodpile beside a steaming kettle of sap hung over an open fire. In a setting of pristine natural beauty, the scene on the label features men gathering sap by hand on snow-covered ground not far from a sugarhouse. A busy interior scene includes the evaporator at center, stacked cordwood, gathering pails on the floor, and two seated figures dimly illuminated through a door and windows. In this cozy sugarhouse, the men recline from their labor while watching the evaporator, that marvel of Yankee ingenuity.

With statements assuring honesty in weight and purity in quality, the label establishes the basic themes of all maple labeling: authenticity, pastoral productivity, healthful outdoor toil, and a clean environment. If maple was to be widely used as a sweetener at the turn of the twentieth century in the face of cheap alternatives, it had to be something that not only satisfied the palate, but invited people into a tradition making them feel good. It's no different today.

· · · · · · ·

THOUGH HE IS long retired and his sugarhouse is in ruins, Wilson "Bill" Clark of Pawlet, Vermont, for over thirty years president of the Vermont association, is the living embodiment of the traditional maple story. Still lanky, but a bit stooped with years of backbreaking labor, he has white hair that seems to float over a face whose liquid blue eyes appear as honest and pure as Vermont's beloved "fancy" grade syrup. Bill has an encyclopedic memory. Whenever we talked, whether at a North American Maple Syrup Council meeting or at his home beside a mud-rutted road, stories poured out in his clipped New England accent as easily as sap into a gathering pail. He not only remembered weather from seasons dating back to the 1940s, but was up on the latest in technology and promotion, and knew how many taps were added to Vermont's production that year. "Most people die of stress," he told me, "and while sugaring gets crazy, it's a great way to burn off a lot of worry. If more folks had a sugarbush, psychologists would need something else to do."

Bill's sugaring career began in 1943 at age twelve when he and his younger brother boiled in a makeshift lean-to, collected sap in forty-quart milk cans on an old one-horse sled, and boiled in a flat pan on a nineteenth-century open stone fire pit they found in the woods. It was a short, lousy season, he recalls, with an early run most producers missed and premature warmth that caused the trees to bud sooner than expected. Two years later, he and his brother built their first sugarhouse with lumber they cut and hauled out of the woods themselves. By that time they had a used evaporator, a new three-barrel gathering tank, and a large storage tank their dad had purchased.

The 1946 season was a good one, he said, leaning back in his chair and seeming to commune with memories as vivid as a dream that startles the sleeper awake. They made seventy gallons of syrup that year, he recollected, leaning forward and out of his reverie.

Neither afraid of new technology nor held in thrall by it, Bill insisted that every sugarmaker on tubing hang a couple of buckets outside his home or sugarhouse, not as a nod to the past or to draw trade like an organ grinder's monkey, but rather to stay in touch with the trees and the season. Looking out his living room window at two beat-up buckets on a stout trunk, he said it was a way to check the daily flow and test for sugar content. He smiled broadly. The buckets also allowed him to take a refreshing draught whenever he wanted and bring back that boyhood excitement from so long ago.

Though he was a taciturn Yankee on most matters, talking maple seemed to induce in Bill a sugaring stream of consciousness about the vicissitudes of weather, incessant equipment tinkering, the joy and rattling exhaustion of the season, and the delight of pleasing people with a product they trusted, including a family that drove all the way from Utica, New York, in 1962 after reading about him in the newspaper. Bill recalled the size and make of every evaporator he had ever used, including a six-foot-by-nineteen-foot behemoth installed in 1958, the largest then in the state. Oil was eleven cents a gallon when he stopped using wood in 1965. Before changing fuels, he'd been burning about eighty-four cords a season. He remembered the details of countless meetings with their seemingly endless discussions and mind-numbing politics about advertising, technology, sugarhouse sanitation, and other issues. True to his reputation, Bill remained a crusader for the "good name of maple," whether it was fighting poor practices of fellow sugarmakers or corporations mislabeling or adulterating products.

In his passion for purity, Bill Clark was a direct descendant of those who formed the association he headed for so long. The "single greatest reason for the formation" of the group, Betty Ann Lockhart wrote in *Maple Sugarin' in Vermont: A Sweet History*, "was the effort to join forces to halt the widespread adulteration of maple products." In 1903, Vermont U.S. senator Redfield Proctor of Burlington, a lover of pure maple syrup and friend of the VMSMA, observed "some of the leading grocers here are making a large display of bottles of 'Towle's Log Cabin Maple Syrup' with a label that identified the company location as Burlington, Vermont and St. Paul Minn."

The senator couldn't "detect any maple taste in this, or very slight." In fact, the syrup Proctor sampled had only a tiny bit of late-season, poor-quality maple for flavoring, and the company had no Vermont presence. In his view, this pretender not only stole business from sugarmakers; it could have the effect of ruining the public's taste for the real thing. The product was the brainchild of grocer Frederick J. Towle, who in 1887 named it in honor of Abraham Lincoln and the legendary log cabin of the president's youth, a deception that no doubt would have been anathema to "Honest Abe."

Proctor became an advocate for a pure food law and wrote passionately to President Theodore Roosevelt on the subject. His efforts bore fruit when the Pure Food and Drug Act became effective on New Year's Day, 1907. Ever since, the law and its amendments have kept Americans safe from a host of contaminated, adulterated, and falsely advertised products. From that time on, at least, the maple world has deferred to Vermont's leadership in safeguarding the purity of the product and authenticity of its story.

· · · · · · · ·

WHEN VERMONT TALKS, maple producers, consumers, and the general public pay attention. For years, one of the principal voices of Vermont maple has been top syrup cop Henry J. Marckres, consumer protection programs chief in the state's Agency of Agriculture, Food and Markets. An easygoing and unassuming man with a mustache and spirited delight in his job, he has been on the maple beat thirty years. Unassailable quality is for Henry the most compelling and essential part of the Vermont maple story, and he considers it an almost sacred duty to protect the brand. The state is also distinguished by a slightly higher sugar density of its product than required elsewhere, the unique and coveted "fancy" designation for light syrup (though it is no longer an official grade), testing of hydrometer accuracy, and vigorous investigation of purity in content and hyperbole in labeling.

Although adulteration is not the problem it was a hundred years ago, Henry remains vigilant about sophisticated, misleading labeling and container design that might fool unwary consumers into confusing "table" or "pancake" syrup for maple. He remembers Log Cabin labels in the 1990s that proclaimed "absolutely pure." It didn't claim to be maple, but the use of "pure" was bound to engender confusion. Eventually, the company changed its label. Another time, a website crowed that the product was "the most authentic syrup, known for its maple taste," though it had little, if any, of the real thing. In 2010, Henry brought to the attention of the federal Food and Drug Administration a product in a maple syrup–style jug that was billed as "all natural" though it contained xanthan gum, caramel color, and just 4 percent maple syrup.

Henry's education in maple began in grammar school when his dad, who ran an auto repair garage, moonlighted by going from farm to farm buying syrup barrels for a wholesaler. In high school, he apprenticed to a sugarmaker in Craftsbury, Vermont, and after college spent a decade as a partner in an operation of eighteen hundred taps running a four-foot-by-fourteen-foot evaporator. Given his experience, he naturally gravitated toward grading and flavor testing maple once he started working for the state.

Henry visits and inspects a lot of sugarhouses and syrup retailers. He is among a few experts running a maple grading school for producers. Mostly he opens syrup containers to ensure color, density, and taste meet legal standards. Tasting syrup sounds like one of those ideal jobs, especially if you have a sweet tooth. But in an ironic twist, Vermont's top syrup cop is a type 2 diabetic and takes extreme care when sampling, watching his diet and other metabolic factors carefully. He once tasted 932 samples in a day, about half a gallon. He won't do that again, but trying as many as a hundred is not unusual.

While he ventures all across the rugged Vermont countryside, the heart of the operation is a small office in a handsome nineteenth-century brick-and-brownstone building on State Street in downtown Montpelier across from the gold-domed state capitol. His cubicle is crowded with papers and reference materials. Included are several shelves of mislabeled or misleading "maple" products that Henry dubs his "wall of shame." Among them is a container of Canadian syrup labeled with the Vermont quality seal, a maple-labeled product that is

Henry Marckres unlocking his basement freezer of off-flavor syrup

merely adulterated sorghum, and a plastic table-syrup jug that repli-
cates the style commonly used by the maple industry.

In the basement, under lock and key, is a feature possessed by no
other government office in the country—a chest freezer filled with
off-flavor maple syrup containers. The syrup is rarely held as evidence. It's used in maple grading classes that Henry teaches, for in-
spector training, and to help producers learn about off flavors. These
flavors include chlorine (sometimes used for cleaning tubing), which
produces "a significant watering of the tongue" and a salty character; metallic tastes from poor-quality barrels or prolonged storage
in metal, which "may affect your teeth like biting a piece of tin foil";
and scorched syrup with a "burned flavor" and "a very strong bite on
the tongue and in the throat." Among other off flavors are musty, fer-
ment, chemical, sour, metabolism, earthy, detergent, those produced
by lubricants and fuels, and "buddy" syrup from sap collected too late
in the season after the buds break on the trees.

While Henry is mild mannered with a policing beat that seems
less risky than most, it can be a dangerous job. It has sent him to the

hospital three times. No, he hasn't been assaulted by sugarmakers for yanking their product off store shelves. In fact, many feel he protects their reputations from possible big mistakes and even lawsuits. It's contaminated syrup that has sent him to the emergency room.

"You never know what you're dealing with," he told me, shaking his head and smiling in recollection. One time he downed the contents of a grading kit, a colored glycerin solution, mistakenly placed in a syrup jug. While investigating an off flavor a few years back, he suddenly turned red and couldn't breathe because the syrup was chemically contaminated when a sugarmaker cleaned his RO with too much sodium hydroxide and the evaporator with phosphoric acid. Another time, a cyanide derivative leaked from a bad gasket.

Even when a visit to the hospital isn't required, syrup sampling has its hazards. After a complaint that syrup bought from a White River Junction gift shop wouldn't come out of the container, Henry picked up a jug and poured it into a glass, only to have it instantly snap back like liquid elastic. He tracked down the packer, who had added water to high-density syrup. Testing revealed that bacteria had consumed all the sugar, leaving a rubbery blob. Another time, he was given a sample with curious, fibrous seeds. It didn't take long to realize that a mouse had made a nest of insulation in the container and that the seeds were turds. "Containers must be inspected before they're used," he said emphatically. "Sometimes you wonder what people are thinking."

Sugarmakers are always experimenting with innovations, but in rare instances common sense is left out of the equation. A producer claimed he had a way to render medium grade out of even the darkest, molasses-looking end-of-season syrup by adding a special chemical to the back pan toward the end of the boil. Word got around and stirred Henry's curiosity. He tested the formulation and found it to have the pH of battery acid.

Marketing the "taste of place" is likely to play a big role in keeping Vermont syrup in the vanguard of the maple world, Henry believes. While he might not be able to tag a particular sample with a specific place, he maintains that soil, depth to bedrock, and other local factors can make for distinctive flavors in syrup, consonant with a concept known as *terroir*. Derived from a French word that means "land," it's a set of special attributes expressed in agricultural products due to the geology, climate, and geography of a place. It's commonly used in connection with wine, coffee, olive oil, beer, chocolate, cheese, and other products that can exhibit distinctive artisanal qualities.

Traditionally, maple syrup tasting deals with color and the detection of off flavors. In the future, according to Henry, syrup will be described by a range of characteristics usable by consumers, including mouth feel, aromatics, and other sensory qualities. These descriptors can be a vehicle for marketing what is special about Vermont syrup. It will promote culinary tourism and support the notion that unique tastes command higher market prices.

In pursuit of a taste-of-place marketing strategy, the "Map of Maple" was created after several years of study by the University of Vermont Nutrition and Food Science Department, Henry's Agency of Agriculture, Food and Markets, and researchers at Middlebury College. Henry handed me a summarized version of the results—a ten-and-a-half-inch-long, brightly colored plastic card dividing maple flavors into eight categories, including toasted, milky, spice, earthy, and fruity. Within each category are several familiar descriptive flavors. For example, under "toasted" the identifying flavors include baked apple, toasted nuts, caramel, and coffee. Among "milky" flavors are butterscotch, condensed milk, and fresh butter. "Spice" includes vanilla, nutmeg, and cinnamon. "Fruity" accounts for raisin, apricot, and peach. The card's back side provides advice on how to taste syrup. It's much like the approach to tasting wine, beginning with a sniff and small sip. Ideally, it's hoped that the Map of Maple will be tied to particular places and sugaring heritage, thereby heightening consumer awareness and willingness to pay a premium.

Henry plans to retire in 2015, and though it will be hard to replace the knowledge and respect he wields, there's no doubt someone in the state will step up and assume the mantle as defender of maple purity, as well as the narrative of honest work and rural simplicity. The tradition in Vermont is too strong for it to be otherwise. While out-of-state maple producers may occasionally be as frustrated at the strong association between syrup and the Green Mountain State as I once was, the benefit of such a connection has extended far beyond Vermont's borders and advantaged sugarmakers everywhere.

Maple Granola

Yield: 7 cups

INGREDIENTS

4 cups rolled oats
2 cups raw wheat germ
1 cup sunflower seeds
1 cup chopped walnuts (add more or less if you'd like)
½ cup shredded coconut (optional)
½ cup dark maple syrup
½ cup canola or olive oil
2 tablespoons vanilla extract
Dried fruit, such as raisins, cranberries, apricots

DIRECTIONS

1. Preheat oven to 300°F.
2. Combine the oats, wheat germ, sunflower seeds, walnuts, and shredded coconut (if using).
3. Mix together the maple syrup, oil, and vanilla and pour over the oat mixture. Stir to combine well.
4. Pour the mixture into a roasting pan and bake at 350°F, periodically stirring with a spatula to prevent sticking, until the mixture dries and is lightly browned, about one hour.
5. Let the mixture cool, then add as much dried fruit as you would like. If adding dried apricots, cut them in quarters before adding to the granola mix.

Recipe by Pat Dubos

Maple Syrup Muffins

Yield: 1 dozen muffins

INGREDIENTS

½ cup maple syrup

Shortening

¼ cup cooking oil

½ cup milk

1 egg

2 cups flour

1 teaspoon salt

3 teaspoons baking powder

Nut Topping (recipe follows)

DIRECTIONS

1. Preheat the oven to 400°F.
2. Grease the bottoms of medium muffin-pan cups with shortening.
3. In a bowl, beat together the maple syrup, oil, milk, and egg with a fork.
4. Sift the dry ingredients into a large bowl and make a well in the center.
5. Pour the liquid into the well in the dry ingredients. Mix quickly and lightly with the fork until all the flour is moistened, but do not beat.
6. Fill each muffin cup two-thirds full. Sprinkle with Nut Topping.
7. Bake the muffins on the rack in the center of the oven for 20–25 minutes or when a cake tester inserted into the center of the muffin comes out clean.

NUT TOPPING

⅓ cup packed brown sugar

½ teaspoon cinnamon

⅓ cup finely chopped nuts

Mix all ingredients together and sprinkle on top of the muffin dough.

Recipe by Shirley Hewlett

The Sweet Experience of Agritainment and Marketing

STATE CAPITAL that it is, Montpelier is nevertheless a small town. It doesn't take long to go from Henry Marckres's office to the rural outskirts and pull into the busy dirt parking lot of Morse Farm Maple Sugarworks, a cluster of dark-brown board-and-batten buildings with red standing-seam metal roofs. The compound sits in a grassy dell at a bend in the road that slows vehicles just enough to get a look at the signs and displays that beckon to tourists. A typical obscure central Vermont dairy farm until the mid-1960s, it was transformed by maple into an internationally known destination visited by ten thousand people annually, including caravans of tour buses. Here plastic tubing inventor Nelson Griggs did much of his research and experimenting in the late 1950s and early 1960s.

Morse's features a woodshed theater, outdoor farm-life museum, chainsaw-carved figures, craft and antique fairs in summer and cross-country ski trails in winter. The real economic engine of the business is the country store, where you can buy any species of maple product in attractive, folksy packaging as well as greeting cards, soaps, candles, foods, coffee, books, dressings, T-shirts, place mats, trivets, lotions, cookie cutters, photos, stuffed animals, and a wide variety of country tchotchkes.

Steam rose from a sugarhouse over a century old on a windy April Fools' Day when I found the ever-genial Burr Morse at the evaporator, the resident demiurge and self-styled "tour guide, jokester, and most visible Vermonter." Partially veiled in mist like the wizard in Dorothy's Oz, he held fourth in Yankee cracker-barrel style, telling two transfixed white-haired Floridians how, while testing the sugar content of syrup in the evaporator, his sleep-deprived dad accidentally poured some down his trousers late one night, hopped quickly out of his pants, and ran out in his skivvies to roll in snow. Like a polished comedian with faultless timing, he had the couple in stitches.

The archetypal New Englander, Burr is a seventh-generation sugar-maker who deftly combines folksiness with the most modern production and business practices. He's quick to spin a yarn, hardworking, and resourceful. He embodies the image created so long ago by the VMSMA and amped by contemporary tourism machinery. Visitors leave feeling they've had a brush with authenticity. Burr knows that the taste of the experience left in the tourists' mind is as important as the flavor of the syrup sample on their tongue.

Harry Morse, his late dad, never much cared for milking cows, Burr told me after the Floridians left. He would tell folks that he didn't like the smell of the barn, and his wife didn't like the smell of him when he came home from the barn, so he decided "to try my hand at milking people." Burr flashed a trademark warm smile. In his mid-sixties, he's a slightly round-faced man with a close-cropped gray beard, a checked shirt, and a baseball-style cap bearing the name of Leader Evaporator. He's got a degree in plant and soil science from the University of Vermont. As a younger man, he never wanted to be a farmer, but he got caught up in his father's enthusiasms. Now he's glad he did.

The decision has also inured to the benefit of Burr's son Tom, an understated and earnest fellow who most enjoys working in the quiet woods setting up and maintaining tubing systems. He's optimistic his preschool daughter will carry Morse Farm sugaring into a ninth generation. Maple teaches perseverance, Tom said, and the capacity to take on multiple tasks, one project, one day at a time. He may lack his father's seemingly easy knack for showmanship, but there's no doubt he will answer the call when the time comes. His passion for teaching people about the land and seasonal cycles is too strong for it to be otherwise.

In 1953, the sugarhouse was taken down board by board and moved here by Burr's grandfather from the ancestral farm not far north. Constructed of weathered gray vertical boards, it has large gaps that let in light and the breeze. Except that it's not in the deep woods, it

Burr Morse spinning a yarn to a couple of Floridians

might as well be the structure depicted on the original 1894 VMSMA label. Visitors like the rustic feel, Burr said.

An ancient sugarhouse, however, does not indicate an old-fashioned operation. Until a few years ago, he still had 150 buckets "for old time sake," but now all thirty-two hundred taps are on vacuum tubing. Tom wants to grow to five to six thousand taps by expanding to rented land a few miles distant. The four- by-twelve-foot evaporator has a Steam-Away and is fueled with a wood-chip gasifier, economical and clean burning; fuel is automatically dropped through a chute from a storage container above. In 2012, Tom installed an RO in anticipation of expansion. Now they make sure to boil during the day so visitors will see, feel, and breathe the slightly flowery fragrance of a steaming sugarhouse. We may trade on the past, Burr acknowledged, but "technology driven by economics has brought sugarin' to a whole new level."

Conversion to wood chips obviated the need to store large amounts of firewood, so Burr converted the woodshed into a theater. Visitors pass through an inviting arched entry, and, flanked by walls of neatly stacked cordwood, sit on stumps and watch a seventeen-minute video of Burr's father telling a tour bus about the sugaring process, including some old-time cuss words and humorous one-liners. He talks about making syrup darker than the inside of a moose and warns that a sugarhouse with a wood-shingle roof is a poor insurance risk. According to Harry, gaps in the sugarhouse siding are not just to enable a parsimonious Yankee to skimp on lumber; they allow incoming air to displace rising steam.

Burr thrives on visitors. They break the monotony. Watching sap boil can be boring and get on the nerves a bit, he admitted. His dad, a nonsmoker, took up the habit a few times during sugaring, as well as gum chewing. But it's quality boredom. Burr is equally deft with a chainsaw or a pen, and slow times in the sugarhouse may be where he gets ideas for the many wood sculptures — animals and human figures — that dot the farm, and for the newspaper columns and books about sugaring and country life that he's written.

Burr shrugged when I asked about the veracity of his tales. They all have "at least one foot in fact," he said, "but bs doesn't always stand for 'best syrup.'" He grinned. "Sugaring is necessary to the personality of a Vermont farm." He might have also added that the personality of the sugarmaker is an essential ingredient in retail sales.

• • • • • • • •

YOU DON'T HAVE TO go to Vermont, visit a big sugarhouse with a gift shop, or spend time with an individual whose family has been making syrup for generations to get an authentic and entertaining experience. Uncle Buck's Sugarhouse is a twenty-by-twenty-four-foot converted garage beside a house on a residential side street in the old mill village of Ashaway, Rhode Island. It may not have the lineage and tourist renown of Morse Farm, but it's just as full of stories and joyful entrepreneurship.

Doing his boiling on his back deck, Tom Buck started in 1996 with a mere five taps. Like so many first-timers, he became hooked, and the next year it was twenty taps on a homemade two-foot-by-four-foot evaporator fueled with propane. "Cost me about $150 a gallon to make the stuff," he laughed. A stout fellow with a welcoming smile, and glasses and mustache, he has worked at industrial machinery builder Davis-Standard in Pawcatuck, Connecticut, for over twenty-five years. He is a licensed pyrotechnician (meaning he shoots off fireworks), doing about ten shows a year, and served as president of the Hopkinton Town Council until he realized budgeting time interfered with the maple season. Instead, he decided to get his dose of politics by founding the Rhode Island Maple Producers Association in 2012. Ever gregarious and engaged in his community, he's thinking of running for council again.

There is an energetic cheer in his tiny sugarhouse, its walls covered with old woodworking tools, decoys, lanterns, snowshoes, and antique maple paraphernalia. We chatted while he ran the evaporator and entertained a steady stream of families with children out on a Sunday to buy candy and syrup. It was busy, and while some people might be frantic or head-down-determined with the crush of activity, Tom took the chaos with a childlike playfulness. His attitude was infectious, and everyone was having fun, swapping stories and drinking up the smell of maple and moisture that filled the place from the roiling boil.

"I'm addicted," Tom said. He went from 150 taps in 2009 to 200 in 2010. Most were on buckets, all from big street and backyard trees. Now he's in the woods running tubing with vacuum on another 125 taps, for a total of 325. Next year he plans to add 200 more taps. He's building an RO of his own design to accommodate the increase.

Tom's uncle Bob, whom he describes as his best friend, is the official assistant sugarmaker and makes maple cream and candy. Tom's eighteen-year-old son collects most of the sap with a truck and gas-powered pump. Steve, a friend whose property has two rows of huge maples with eighty buckets, is the unofficial taste tester. "I like sugaring," Steve said archly, "because it keeps me out of trouble spending money in bars." Despite the levity, he's serious about sugaring. One night his girlfriend called with an amorous invitation that he refused because he and Tom were in the midst of a long boil.

Tom delights in marketing and has a knack for publicity. He's got an attractive, photocopied brochure and is good at old-fashioned word-of-mouth merchandising. Before he started working third shift, he'd call a local television station regularly to talk about the weather and how the sap was running. A couple of stations have recently done stories on his operation. He gets school groups, including urban kids from Providence, as well as an occasional busload of seniors.

The sugarhouse is a kind of town hall annex, and Tom delighted in holding forth with citizens and public officials who came by to talk politics. The police chief, a stocky former state trooper with a gray crew cut, popped in as I was on my way out. He refused a bag of maple popcorn because it's so good he's afraid he won't be able to stop eating until he has a stomachache, like last time. He and Tom traded good-natured barbs. "Watch out," the officer teased, "or I'm going to start a rumor that you buy your syrup from a big box store."

• • • • • • • •

IF YOU THINK OF all sugarmakers as gray-bearded backwoodsmen or people with big families who pitch in gathering sap, then you haven't met Ben Fisk of Temple, New Hampshire. He's a young dynamo whose website proclaims him "New Hampshire's King of Maple Syrup." His sugaring career began at age five following a preschool class visit to a sugarhouse. He was mesmerized, could think of nothing but maple afterward. The next day his contractor father, who had made syrup in the past, fabricated a barrel evaporator for Ben and began tutoring him in the art. With buckets borrowed from his grandfather, also a former sugarmaker, he made less than a gallon. The following Christmas, Ben's dad gave him a two-foot-by-six-foot evaporator and built him a small sugarhouse. With help from his dad and a neighbor, he made thirty-eight gallons on 250 taps.

In 2004 at age fifteen, Ben took first place at the Cheshire and Hillsborough County Fairs for his medium amber syrup. Entered into the Carlisle competition at the New Hampshire Maple Producers Association, it won the trophy for best syrup. That year he also won the association's Felker Award, given to encourage youngsters in the maple business. A black-and-white photo of him holding the plaque reveals a stocky boy with chubby cheeks beneath a baseball-style cap. When I first met him he was twenty-one, tall and muscular, and already had two sugarhouses. One was beside the family home in Temple, the other in Newberry, New Hampshire. His operations had almost two thousand taps and employed two people full time during the season.

By age twenty-six, he had grown into a strapping fellow, with stubble on his cheeks. He had about fifteen thousand taps in 2013, eighteen thousand in 2014, and was confident of twenty-one thousand in 2015. Ten full-time employees did everything from paperwork to candy making and working in the woods. During the season two additional people are on the payroll.

Ben's plan is to add three to four thousand taps per year for as long as he can. "There are trees all over the place," he said. "Maybe I'll do that for the next fifty years." In 2014 he produced forty-five hundred gallons of syrup, but that represented only 10 percent of what he sold. Like many larger producers, he purchases syrup wholesale and repackages it or makes it into other products, like candy.

Since childhood, Ben has possessed a ferocious work ethic, an indomitable entrepreneurial spirit, and a drive that accepts nothing short of success. It's inspiring. Even the most eager overachiever can be forgiven for feeling lazy in his presence. He remembers high school teachers who warned him he'd never make a living from maple and delights in proving them wrong every day. Like any sugarmaker, he's had setbacks. A few years ago, an ice storm tore down his tubing, and wildfire once ripped through his Newberry bush, melting a couple of acres of lines. He didn't get discouraged.

"I want to be the state's largest producer," he told me. Then he paused, as if listening to a private cheerleader. "Maybe I'll be the biggest in the world," he added. His ambition is to have a year-round business like Bruce Bascom, whom he admires and from whom he has bought a good deal of syrup and equipment. He envisions a chain of sugarhouses known for product excellence and school educational programs. He talks about operating a pancake house and raising bees.

Ben is a natural marketer. He's articulate, persuasive, and "into branding." He likes hobnobbing at trade shows. In 2014, he came out with a color catalog. Ben designed a green label for "Award Winning" syrup that includes a bit of his personal narrative and the tag line "tapped just for you." He doesn't use the standard New Hampshire labeled jugs because it promotes the state, not his business. He's got a colorful website from which he sells not only syrup but candy, sugar, fudge, maple cotton candy, maple cream, maple-bacon lollipops, barbecue sauce, maple drops, pancake mix, maple coffee, wedding favors, and a variety of gifts. His syrup is used in McCrea's Tapped Maple Caramels.

Ben has persuaded over one hundred farms, gift shops, gas stations, general stores, supermarkets, cafés, and other retailers in three states to carry his products. Ben's maple syrup is on the shelves in Hannaford supermarkets and can be found at Marshalls, T. J. Maxx, HomeGoods, and other retailers. He goes to about fifty fairs, craft sales, shows, and other events annually. Halfway through 2014, sales were up 40 percent over the previous year. Ever since his teens he's garnered a lot of press, and was featured in *Yankee* in 2013. That same year, Fox News labeled Ben's one of the "top ten American sugar shacks."

Ben is excited by what he does, is in thrall to sugaring. "After all these years, I still enjoy every day," he told me. Visitors feel the energy, and it rouses their interest in the product.

Ben is always looking to make his operation more efficient. Long using vacuum tubing and RO, he recently went from a wood-fired evaporator to oil and added a semiautomatic bottling line that can do one hundred pints in half an hour. Explosive growth, however, has left the business in a series of small buildings, all bursting at the seams with materials and activity and surrounded by a jumble of tanks, tubing, pallets, barrels, and other items. The neat, orderly salesroom could use more shelves, the candy-making area is squeezed into a narrow room near the RO machines, it's tight around the evaporator, and the office and bottling lines are in separate buildings.

In autumn 2013, Ben bought fifteen acres along New Hampshire Route 101 down the street from his home and first sugarhouse. He's putting up a farm stand in 2014 to sell maple products as well as breads and garden crops, including corn, for which he has high hopes as a wholesale item. A new post-and-beam sugarhouse will go up in 2015, if financing works out. He envisions fifteen hundred square feet with a separate evaporator room so tours can be given without interfering with other parts of the operation. His new five-foot-by-fourteen-foot evaporator is cramped in the current sugarhouse but will have plenty of space in the new one. Behind the new building he is planning a one-thousand-square-foot packaging facility with bottling lines, candy-making space, and storage for syrup and other products.

There will be a spacious gift shop, interior sap tanks, and a loading dock for big trucks. The building will be expandable on all sides.

A far-off look came into his face, as if he were constructing the new building in his mind as we spoke. He smiled. "We put a lot into the product," he said.

• • • • • • • •

SAY THE WORDS "maple syrup" while discussing good eats, and the first thing that comes to mind is pancakes. Say "pancake" and instantly thoughts run to syrup. So it's not surprising that pancake restaurants were one of the earliest and still most successful maple-related businesses pursued by sugarmakers beyond syrup production. Like syrup making, they are frequently multigenerational family operations, often along busy roads and seasonally open. Their patrons are fiercely loyal, returning year after year for a good meal and a family kitchen atmosphere.

Mouthwatering Finnish pancakes smothered in dark amber syrup lured my wife Mary and me to Davenport Maple Farm in Shelburne, Massachusetts, on a blustery March Sunday. It's not the oldest of its kind, nor is it the only one in the area. There's another sugarhouse restaurant ten minutes away and more than a dozen within a half-hour drive, but Davenport's is emblematic of all that is best in such places. Besides, there are few eateries where you can get Finnish pancakes, a kind of marriage of soufflé and French toast with the texture of bread pudding.

We drove north from Connecticut on I-91 and got off at Greenfield, Massachusetts, on State Route 2, dubbed "the Mohawk Trail," climbing into the hill country west of the Connecticut River. Soon we took a right onto a narrow road where thick forest growing to the pavement's edge was interrupted by just a few houses. We passed a few maple groves, some with buckets on the trees. The road continued to curve and rise until we arrived at a cleared high point in a burst of light and space from which a cluster of houses was visible among fields, and then a group of barns, a blue silo, and Davenport's sugarhouse with welcoming steam rising. All was set in a bowl below low, wooded hills.

Built into a hillside, the sugarhouse is a long building of dark vertical boards topped by a red standing-seam roof. The sugaring operation is on the lower floor, with the fifty-seat, knotty-pine-paneled restaurant above. The place was buzzing, and with a forty-minute wait for breakfast, we got our names on the restaurant list and went to hang out in the warm, moist, and slightly sweet-smelling sugarhouse, where the sound of the boil mixed with the hum of visitors talking. I quickly spotted family patriarch Russ Davenport, who grew up on this farm his grandfather bought in 1913, and grabbed the seat next to him. The family began sugaring here in 1914, he told me, though maple has been made on the property since 1772. Moving around in a wheelchair with practiced ease, Russ is a big man with gray hair, wearing heavy glasses and a plaid shirt. He is one of the grand old men of sugaring, known for an excellent product, his integrity, and hard work. The sugarhouse features a wall of ribbons testifying to the quality of his syrup, and he's served on all manner of maple industry committees and panels.

Like many sugarmakers, Russ delights in telling stories and has a laconic, down-home charm that holds the attention of visitors. He talked about working with Bob Lamb on his early tubing experiments, and with plastic jug innovators Elmer Kress and Charles Bacon, who taught him that it takes some failure to be successful. "Do you cause the rain or learn to dance?" he asked, pointing a finger. He has spent a lot of time testing various maple products, like nuts and cranberries. I suppose he did a lot of dancing before rain began falling.

The two-story walls of the sugarhouse are tattooed with Russ's maple antiques — buckets, tubing, molds, spiles, carrying yokes, and all manner of syrup containers. Not just proud of maple history, he has lived it. Born in 1929, he remembers wooden-stave buckets with metal hoops and collecting with horses, which didn't end until 1964. Now he's at home with an oil-fired evaporator, RO, and vacuum tubing, enjoying being the farm's spokesman while his son Norman does the sugaring.

When they opened the restaurant in 1990, Russ told me, it wasn't because they needed more to do. Rather, he wanted the farm to sustain more of the family. A look of deep satisfaction glowed on his work-worn face as he told me that his wife Martha, an elegant woman with a warm smile, works the counter, while Norm's wife Lisa and their daughter Meagan run the kitchen and daughter Dina works as head waitress. Norm's sister helps during the season, as do many other family members. As we sat and talked, Russ's grandson Fred ran the evaporator. It's that feeling of being part of an extended family that lures customers, that imbues them with the maple story, a significant ingredient in the sweet taste of syrup.

Our names were called by a mustachioed older man in a red vest, and I said goodbye to Russ. As I left, he mentioned that former governor William Weld and comedian Bill Cosby and other celebrities had had meals at the tables upstairs. Mary and I walked out of the sugarhouse and upslope along the side of the building to the restaurant. Open from eight in the morning until three in the afternoon, even now at a little past one and beyond the prime time for breakfast or Sunday brunch it was crowded with customers eating family style at long tables. The room was rich with the smell of sizzling pancakes and irresistible bacon. The homey sound of dishes clanking and forks scraping on plates mixed with the hum of conversation. Almost as soon as we sat down a waitress poured coffee into our mugs, part of an eclectic collection in all colors, designs, and logos.

It was late enough to have had a lunch of hamburgers made from the farm's cattle, but we wanted something to pour syrup on, so I ordered the Finnish pancakes, and Mary had French toast with sausage; each order was delivered with a tiny plastic bottle of maple. While we sipped our coffee and watched the rhythm of staff in red shirts dash around the room, we fell into conversation with the couple next to us, who had driven about as far but from another direction. They were considering some backyard sugaring, and I gladly fielded their questions, with a warning about maple addiction. In Davenport's welcoming atmosphere we quickly kindled a warm if ephemeral friendship. After our meal was delivered and while shoveling delicious forkfuls of food that felt as satisfying as that served in a neighbor's kitchen, we continued talking about our children, some recent art shows, and concerts we'd seen. Smiles led to laughter. By the time we had left, both our stomachs and our souls were satisfied. The day seemed somehow brighter, more promising.

• • • • • • •

COMMEMORATION AND celebration that honor personalities and achievements are organic to any community, and the world of sugarmakers is no exception. The universe of maple has a host of festivals, museums, and open sugarhouse events, as well as year-round gift shops that trumpet the industry. Much of it is a species of marketing that keeps maple in the public mind and recounts the nostalgic narrative first articulated in an organized manner by the VMSMA in the late nineteenth century.

The International Maple Hall of Fame at the American Maple Museum, founded in 1977 in the small town of Croghan, New York, just west of the Adirondacks, is a little different. While the museum portion of the facility displays a lot of equipment and, like similar institutions, tells the sugaring story for public edification, the hall of fame section is a room more meaningful to sugarmakers themselves.

The museum is housed in an old brick school building donated by Bob Lamb and his wife Florence, and in the basement is a room featuring a Cooperstown-like shrine with plaques and photographs of those who have been inducted into the hall of fame in honor of their contribution to the industry. With little else in the room but photographed faces, some smiling and some sober, the effect was arresting. There are not only sugarmakers, but scientists, inventors, writers, and equipment manufacturers. Of the more than eighty members, about a third are New Englanders. Many were familiar to me, including Mike Girard, Bruce Bascom, and Bill Clark. Others were legends I'd only heard about. With some, it was my first introduction. Regardless, through sugaring I shared a fundamental experience with all of them. It almost seemed like a gallery of family portraits that included distant relatives I'd never met.

Among the Yankees in the hall of fame is Russ Davenport, enshrined in 1986. The maple world may be spread halfway across the northern part of the continent, but in human terms it's a relatively small circle, and despite distance many sugarmakers know each other. There's an unusually high degree of empathy among them forged by the vicissitudes of seasons, hard work, and conviviality at meetings. Many sugarmakers look at each other not as colleagues and certainly not rivals, but as family. When Russ talked to me about Charles Bacon, Bob Lamb, and Elmer Kress, all hall-of-famers who have passed away, he grew misty, as one might for a beloved cousin or sibling. I think he was wiping a tear when he leavened the moment with humor and remarked that "old sugarmakers never die, they just evaporate."

The highest honor afforded by the maple industry, election recognizes "those who have excelled in research, development and leadership." Typically, two people are added each year by vote of the North American Maple Syrup Council. A ceremony is conducted on the third Saturday in May, kicked off by a big pancake breakfast prepared by volunteers. Afterward, there's lots of maple schmoozing and an opportunity to wander the museum brimming with tools, equipment, and artifacts from across the maple world. Equipment dealers and crafters pitch colorful tents on the lawn, giving the day a festival atmosphere.

Like many maple events, induction day has an old-fashioned, bottled-in-amber quality. The pancake breakfast is served family-style at long tables, where familiar faces gather and new friends are made. There's no need searching for a topic of conversation to break the ice. Everyone is acquainted by common experience and interest. An all-you-can-eat meal includes stacks of fluffy pancakes and bowls of sausage and ham chunks. Syrup is served in pint plastic jugs. It's a relaxed, convivial atmosphere in a room where light from tall windows is filtered through curtains bearing a colorful maple-leaf motif. American and Canadian flags hang in the long rectangular space. Though I knew very few people and Mary knew no one when we attended in 2014, we felt at ease, welcomed.

Following breakfast, we witnessed the crowning of the New York State maple queen and maple princess. Several anxious but nevertheless poised teens dressed in colorful prom-style dresses gave short speeches about their involvement with maple and what they would do, if chosen, to promote the industry at fairs and other events. If it was at all a beauty contest, it seemed more about inner beauty, about someone who will not only attract attention but radiate the values prized in the maple world—purity, naturalness, honesty. Both the oratory and crowning ceremony by the reigning monarchs had a rural sweetness taking one back a few generations to simpler times. Neither Mary nor I picked the winners, but the judges' choices were sound.

After the maple royalty had their moments, the hall of fame inductees, introduced with affection, took center stage. Their accomplishments were described by industry leaders who knew them personally. Jacques Couture of Westfield, Vermont, a sugarmaker and dairy farmer with a long record of civic involvement, was introduced by Leader Evaporator president Gary Gaudette. Publicists, writers, and filmmakers Don and Betty Ann Lockhart were presented by David Marvin, a friend who is one of the largest and most innovative sugarmakers in the business. Each of the inductees was handed a plaque and a pin by Gaudette and then said a few words, usually of thanks for all who helped them along the way, including their families. It was a surprisingly emotional moment, and I felt a lump in my throat, as if I had had some direct involvement instead of being merely a spectator. I'd only met these newly minted members of the hall that day, yet I felt a connection. I was not alone in my mood, and the sentiment in the room was palpable.

The maple exhibits in Croghan have the homey and sometimes hokey feel of a beloved small-town historical society museum that has accepted an eclectic collection of donated artifacts and done its best to create a coherent story. Many of the objects are valuable antiques, from wooden-stave buckets to the earliest evaporators.

Maple museums vary in quality. I'm sure that such attractions satisfy the casual tourist's curiosity, but anyone with a deep interest ought to visit one of the many sugarhouses where antique tools of the trade are displayed. Whether at Davenport's in Massachusetts, Morse's in Vermont, Clark's in New Hampshire, or myriad other places where maple is made, the curious traveler can witness actual sugaring and hear stories of veteran maple people enlivening the antique paraphernalia on walls and shelves. Even out of season, visiting a real operation like these teaches more than a museum's static displays.

Housed in a gray, barnlike building along U.S. Route 7, the New England Maple Museum in Pittsford, Vermont, bills itself as "exciting and educational," with "the most complete collection of sugaring artifacts in existence." Indeed, there are many fascinating and valuable antiques under one roof that are the envy of any collector. Unfortunately, many of these genuine historical objects are elaborated by fusty murals and dioramas illustrating a saccharine nostalgia. Furthermore, when I visited near the end of sugaring season 2013, hay bales and stereotypical Yankee mannequins freighted the exhibits with more kitsch than the artifacts could reasonably sustain.

For fifteen bucks, visitors received a heavy dose of romantic yearning as they learned that "maple syrup does not continuously flow from the tree into the can and onto the shelf." The modern equipment displays, including a working oil-fired evaporator, were not so modern. Although tubing was covered, there was not a word about RO. Nothing was mentioned about current trends, opportunities, challenges, and threats to the maple industry, recent nutritional discoveries, or environmental stewardship. It appeared little had been updated for more than five years, and very little then.

The museum portion of the building contrasted with the well-lit and attractively displayed gift shop through which a visitor both entered and exited. It was chock-full of syrup, candy, and other products, but much of the space was given over to stuffed animals, cosmetics, toys, trash cans, caps, T-shirts, and knickknacks that have no maple connection. It felt like a classic tourist trap.

· · · · · · · ·

AS THE SEASON hits its stride—mid-March for southern New England and late April in the far north—maple celebrations abound. It's possible that no other agricultural product enjoys so many commemorative events. Observances can be as big as the three-day Vermont Maple Festival in St. Albans, with exhibits, an antiques show, outdoor entertainment, road race, talent show, carnival rides, children's games, buffet dinner, and parade. Or they can be as simple as opening local sugarhouses to the public, as the Gill, Massachusetts, Agricultural Commission once did, or sponsoring a sugaring documentary movie and discussion, something they now do biennially.

Some maple events hallow history. Among them is the annual Native American sugaring demonstration at the Institute for American Indian Studies in Washington, Connecticut, where sap is boiled by using heated rocks. Another is the early nineteenth-century kettle-style Maple Days at Old Sturbridge Village in Sturbridge, Massachusetts.

Although maple festivals were intended originally to bring attention to the industry and sell some local syrup, many events have become significant area tourism generators. The promoters may not even have connections to the maple industry. Not far from where I live, a suburban hotel has advertised a "March–Maple Tree Hugger Package" that included a studio suite with breakfast, a jug of maple syrup, and a map of local sugarhouses that give tours—all starting at $135 for two. With every booking, the hotel promised to donate "$10 to the Arbor Foundation" in the customer's name and send "a certificate . . . to commemorate your gift." Oddly, the photos in the advertising package depicted birches. "Come celebrate maple season with us and help the earth!" a flyer crowed.

For the novice who wants to learn about sugaring or the veteran aficionado who wants to reconnect with the sources of his or her delight, nothing beats a small-town maple festival. It's not only an opportunity for sugarmakers to sell syrup and visitors to experience the magic of sugaring, but a time for a community to get together after the isolation of winter. Close to my Connecticut home I have a special affection for the Hebron Maple Festival, which will celebrate its twenty-fifth year in 2015. Not only are there a few sugarhouses open to the public, but the festival includes a Girl Scout cookie sale, a church craft fair, food from local veterans, face painting and other children's activities, firehouse tours with sugar on snow, a women's club pet boutique, kettle corn at the bank, a Knights of Columbus pancake breakfast, s'mores made by Cub Scouts, and one-room-schoolhouse tours by the historical society. It is the largest event of its kind in the state, mobilizing the entire town by maple, and has become a big part of Hebron's identity, even though the town does not have Connecticut's biggest producers, the most sugarhouses, or the largest maple orchards.

For its rural, small-town charm and wide range of sugaring operations, the annual festival in Whitingham, Vermont, held in late March is among the most vibrant and fun. Situated between Bennington and Brattleboro and about twenty-five miles north of Greenfield,

Massachusetts, Whitingham (notable historically as the birthplace of Brigham Young) is a town of about thirteen hundred people, within which is the community of Jacksonville, a mill village ensconced in a narrow stream valley. The two-day festival is the town's defining event and "an important aspect of Whitingham's economic and cultural heritage," according to the festival brochure. Sugarhouse visiting opportunities typically feature everything from a ten-thousand-tap operation with a large RO system in spacious modern quarters to a farm that uses draft horses to collect sap from eight hundred buckets.

The day begins, in typical festival manner, with a pancake breakfast at the municipal center in Jacksonville, a cluster of houses at the junction of State Routes 100 and 112. There is a white church with a clock tower, a gas station, a general store that looks much like a large house, and the old clapboard municipal center—sheltering the library and town offices—next to a brick firehouse. Across the road is a long wooden factory building identified as the state's first butter plant. The breakfast is in a wainscoted hall with a hardwood floor and a large, colorful mural illustrating a farmer working with draft horses. The hall was warm and humming with conversation, its long tables filled with families. There was a line when I got there at nine o'clock. Everyone seemed to know each other, and there was talk about the snowy weather, school sports, someone's logging operation.

On Route 100 up the hill and out of the valley, Whitingham Elementary School/Twin Valley Middle School was holding a craft fair spread on long tables in the vast echoing gym. Outside in the parking lot, a couple of chilled but cheerful elderly women were sitting in a boxy information booth, a trailer made to look like a small sugarhouse. A moderate snow was blowing in horizontal bands as we chatted. Last year, they complained lightheartedly, temperatures were in the seventies, trees were budding, and the season was ending. Now the season was starting slowly, the snow was deep, and the sap hadn't run much.

My first stop was at Sprague and Son Sugarhouse, where I got a hearty greeting from Marty Sprague, a fit man with a thick mustache. The sugarhouse was a vertically sided, unpainted, barnlike structure with two stacks and a cupola. It's a relatively new building, the Spragues having decided to move the old family operation closer to the main road to attract trade. The evaporator gleams near the middle of the structure, and a sales counter occupies a corner. Part of the sugarhouse is an old church built by Carthusian monks in the middle of the last century. Marty had the structure moved in several pieces, and pointed out where the altar once was. In his early twenties, Marty's son Rodney is a sixth-generation sugarmaker. When he was younger, it was his job to gather sap from the beauty buckets across the street. It was a task he hated so much that he once asked his dad if he could punch holes in the bottoms so he wouldn't have to bother collecting.

The largest sugaring operation in Whitingham, with over ten thousand taps, is Corse Farm, on a narrow road bounded by fields and forest and punctuated by a few houses. Sugaring is done in a collection of connected, vertically sided buildings, one of which is open-ended and filled with cordwood. The massive six-by-twenty-foot wood-fired evaporator is in a spacious room that rises two and a half stories to the ceiling. It's joined via a hallway to a heated finishing and sales room with shelves of syrup jugs for sale, a canner, sink, and long counter. In a small room off the hall is the RO.

The evaporator room was busy with people marveling at the stainless behemoth, sampling the farm's cheese on toothpicks and maple milkshakes in small paper cups. A crowd of families with young children was gathered around a plywood panel hanging on the wall. It listed production records dating to 1918, including cryptic annotations about new equipment or changes in technique.

A man in a tan jumpsuit named Leon gave tours of the evaporator when enough people asked. Though eager and cheerful, he confessed not to know everything because he runs the dairy end of the farm. His brother is the sugarmaker and designed the evaporator, custom fabricated to conduct two separate boils simultaneously. Thus, sap from tubing is handled separately from bucket sap, which he said tends to be darker.

A large, technologically up-to-date operation, Corse Farm goes back to 1868. But despite its scale and thoroughly modern atmosphere, it retained the old-timey sense of a family operation. I felt more as if I'd entered someone's home than a production facility.

A rickety shack with eclectic windows and doors, and gaps in the vertical siding through which sunlight and breezes easily pass, the Bemis Sugarhouse on State Route 8A seemed at first glance a throwback in time, the opposite of Corse Farm. With its rusting metal roof and uneven wooden floor, it gave the impression, at least at first, of a distant era. But in its use of vacuum tubing for most taps, RO, and an oil-fired evaporator, it was contrastingly modern. In its family atmosphere, it was timeless.

Bemis Sugarhouse is a four-generation operation, and the resident spirit of the place is Bud, billed in the tour materials as "a real Vermonter" glad to tell visitors about the "good ole days." He's a big, older man with a classic flat Yankee accent who retains a bit of a baby face. His wife is a warm, white-haired woman who had meticulously set out syrup samples, cookies she baked, and maple-coated walnuts. She urged me to sample as much as I wanted, and my pleasure in tasting the delectables may have been exceeded only by the pleasure she got out of watching me enjoy. She seemed like grandmother incarnate.

Bud took delight in showing me around the evaporator. The arch is ancient, though they don't know how old because they bought it already well used in 1973. After detailing how his system operated, he motioned toward an old newspaper photo on the wall. It showed his dad sugaring in 1962. He turned to me and, sure he had my full attention, said, "The first thing you do to be successful at making syrup"—as his father told him—"is to get your mind set that you are not going to make any money."

Bud's comment was less about surrendering any hope of income from sugaring than it was an emphasis on what was most important: community, family, a lifestyle that bent to a changing season. These are the things that are essential to what sugarmakers sell and customers eagerly buy, perhaps the finest, sweetest product produced in sugarhouses everywhere, certainly in any worth a visit. Spend time in Whitingham's sugarhouses and you'll find the real flavor of maple is less about a pancake topping and recipe ingredient than the feel of the landscape, awareness of weather, and the sugarmaker's approach to life.

Applesauce Maple Loaf

Yield: 16–18 half-inch to one-inch cake slices

INGREDIENTS

½ cup unsalted butter
½ cup maple sugar
1 large egg
¼ cup maple syrup
½ teaspoon maple flavoring
1½ cups all-purpose flour
2 cups whole-wheat flour
½ teaspoon baking soda
1 teaspoon baking powder

1 teaspoon ground cinnamon
¾ teaspoon ground nutmeg
½ teaspoon ground cloves
½ teaspoon salt
1½ cups applesauce
½ cup raisins or dried
    cranberries
½ cup chopped walnuts
Maple Glaze (optional)

DIRECTIONS

1. Preheat the oven to 350°F.
2. Cream the butter and maple sugar until light.
3. Beat in the egg, maple syrup, and maple flavoring; stop the mixer and scrape the sides and bottom of the bowl.
4. Whisk together the flour, baking soda, baking powder, cinnamon, nutmeg, cloves, and salt.
5. Gradually add the flour to the creamed mixture.
6. Beat the applesauce into the batter.
7. Stir in the raisins and nuts.
8. Place in a greased and floured 9-by-5-inch loaf pan. Bake for 1 hour, until a tester inserted in the center comes out clean.
9. Remove from the oven and cool on a rack in the pan for 10 minutes. Remove from pan and finish cooling on the rack before serving. If you like, you can top the cooled loaf with Maple Glaze.

Maple Glaze

INGREDIENTS

1 cup sifted confectioners' sugar
¼ teaspoon maple syrup
2 to 4 tablespoons heavy cream

DIRECTIONS

Whisk ingredients together until smooth. Drizzle over cooled loaf.

Recipe by Midge Harvey

Maple Nut Blueberry Muffins

Yield: 1 dozen muffins

INGREDIENTS

2 cups flour
2 teaspoons baking powder
1 tablespoon maple sugar
¼ cup maple syrup
1 stick butter, melted
¼ cup milk
2 eggs, beaten
1½ cups blueberries
¼ cup chopped nuts

DIRECTIONS

1. Preheat oven to 375°F.
2. In a large bowl, mix together flour, baking powder, and maple sugar. Set aside.
3. Spray a 1-cup glass measuring cup with cooking spray. Measure the maple syrup into the cup. To this, add the butter. Melt in microwave on high for about 1 minute, watching carefully. When the butter is mostly melted, remove from the microwave and continue stirring until totally melted.
4. In another bowl, add the butter mixture to the milk. Then add this wet mixture to the flour mixture and add the two beaten eggs. Mix well.
5. Fold in the blueberries and nuts.
6. Spray muffin tin with cooking spray. Fill each muffin two-thirds full.
7. Sprinkle the tops of the muffins with some maple sugar before baking.
8. Bake at 375°F for 20−25 minutes, or until they test done. Cool in pan for 10 minutes before moving muffins to a cooling rack.

Recipe by Kirsten Walker

Family,
····· Community, ·····
Tradition

ABOUT SIXTY PEOPLE, mostly children with their elders, gathered around Roaring Brook Nature Center's Jay Kaplan as he drilled a taphole in a large roadside maple using a battered carpenter's brace. The mustachioed Kaplan, who has headed the Canton, Connecticut, center for decades, is a talented old-style naturalist with a knack for engaging kids. His easy manner and ironic wit also keep adults attentive. Each March he runs a demonstration that includes a brief lecture on maple identification and the sugaring process, followed by actual tree tapping and sap boiling. Interest is growing, he believes, because sugaring makes people feel less suburban and more connected to the land. For more than a dozen years, he's asked me to join him, run the primitive outdoor evaporator, and explain how sap becomes syrup.

It was a cool, sunny day, and everyone was bundled in brightly colored ski jackets or heavy wool coats. Though I was standing almost fifty feet away, I knew the sap was running by the sigh that issued from the crowd like a collective breath as Jay inserted a galvanized spile in the hole he had just drilled. Most of the group then lined up and stuck out a finger for a drop they could taste before walking over to where I stood beside the evaporator. Though my bad back threw me into early retirement as a sugarmaker, I wouldn't want to miss this yearly event, which fills me with endorphins of happy memories generated by the amazed expressions on the faces of these sugaring innocents. Some people might think there's not much excitement in watching sap boil, but from this small crowd I feel a palpable "cool" factor, something registering high on the "wow" index.

Stoked with chunks of wood by a teenage volunteer, the evaporator is a rusting thirty-five-gallon drum on its side. There's an opening in the bung end for fuel and a square hole on top where a shallow, flat tin pan full of sap is placed in front of a short metal exhaust pipe. The rig is hauled from a storage shed each year and set up in the driveway, puffing steam and smoke to the delight of the children who are watched carefully by parents, fearful the little ones might want to touch the hot contraption. While everyone stood mesmerized as if I presided over the witches' cauldron in *Macbeth*, I explained how sap is handled and boiled, when to tell it's syrup by use of a hydrometer or thermometer, about filtering, and what the different colors of syrup mean.

When I'm done talking, I never fail to cajole the group into telling me the most important thing to know about sugaring. I invariably hear shout-outs from both adults and kids. Keep the stored sap cool, some say. Others repeat what I just told them about watching the pan so it won't boil dry. There's always a youngster proud to warn everyone not to get burned. "No," I tell them, "the most important thing to know about sugaring is to have fun." I ask the question again, even louder, and get about forty children shouting back a very satisfying, "have fun."

Bread for dipping into syrup and coffee made with sap provide a few social moments after the demo and time for questions. A couple in their thirties thought sugaring was something playful and interesting they could do with their kids. A husky middle-aged fellow in a navy peacoat told me he lived in the barn of what was once a farm. "I want to channel the farm," he said, "reconnect." A twenty-something with a toddler in tow eagerly related remembrances of her late grandfather sugaring. Like Proust with his madeleines, for her the smell of boiling sap opened vast worlds of past experience. As a means of getting closer to her grandfather, even in death, she wanted to try it herself.

Maple draws an amazing range of people with diverse interests. As I packed up some sample filters and a grading kit, an elderly man with a nimbus of white hair tugged my sleeve. "There are trees in my backyard," he said, "and I'm curious." His daughter, a slender, dark-haired woman standing next to him and holding a baby, looked at me,

Jay Kaplan teaches

then the child, and back at me. "I want food that's pure and made the old-fashioned way," she said.

A few years back I met Rand Richards Cooper at Roaring Brook, an author and critic who has been a travel writer for *Bon Appétit*. He thought interest in sugaring was growing with the "slow food" movement and a desire for tastes that are authentically local. While attending a Massachusetts college years ago, he and some friends tapped a few trees at the edge of campus. "It seemed a crazy, wild thing to do, atavistic and almost pagan," as they boiled sap over a bonfire with a bunch of other rowdy students. It wasn't your typical beery collegiate night, because the next morning they had a couple of smoky pints of syrup instead of hangovers.

· · · · · · ·

IT MIGHT HAVE BEEN a program like Roaring Brook's that first hooked Geoff Picard on sugaring when his dad took him to a demonstration at age twelve. In his thirties, Picard is not a big man, but wiry and strong. He's a natural teacher who excites students with the sugarhouse he runs at Lyman High School in rural Lebanon, Connecticut.

The small structure was built in 2010 with a power company grant, and I approached with a touch of nostalgia as it emitted a plume of steam into a cerulean March sky. Inside was the two-foot-by-four-foot evaporator I'd bought years earlier and used to make as much as fifty gallons of syrup a season. I had donated it to the school earlier that year along with taps, buckets, storage tanks, a canner, hydrometers, filters, and all the other tackle and trim of sugaring. On an icy January day, Geoff had come to my house with two burly students and a flatbed truck. They loaded it all in less than twenty minutes, and years of sugaring memories went down the road. I felt as if I'd lost a part of my life, a sense of my self.

That feeling of loss returned as I approached the small, cupola-topped structure where a few students in bright coats and blue jeans lingered. But the feeling evaporated instantly as I entered and saw the old familiar pan aboil again, with youngsters busy about the arch drawing off and filtering syrup. A blond ponytailed girl checked the density with my hydrometer; a stubble-cheeked boy in an orange watch cap skimmed foam off the evaporator with my long-handled stainless scoop. I was glad to be there, happy to have played a role in teaching these kids, perpetuating the tradition. Over the years, I'd developed a relationship with this steaming, fire-breathing metal machine and felt good I hadn't just traded it for cash. My relationship now extended to these kids, who thanked me profusely and were eager to show me what they were doing.

Geoff has integrated sugaring into his forestry curriculum. That first year, when I visited, they made about a gallon of syrup. Since then they've made as much as ten gallons. Most of it is given away, with enough saved for a pancake breakfast honoring young future farmers. His class of about a dozen helps tap and collect sap. Occasionally they boil during school hours, but mostly it's after classes. The kids like hanging out and chopping wood. Sometimes he'll buy a pizza, or they cook hot dogs in the boiling sap. Even graduates return to help.

For Geoff, sugaring is like a vacation from the usual routines of life, and he wants his students to share that spirit of doing something special. He prefers to look at it as a hobby, like fishing. That way, it doesn't get tiring and oppressive, as a business can. He wants kids who grew up getting their food from the supermarket to understand all the hard work that goes into producing something to eat. It's a sensory process they can see, smell, touch, and taste. "That's what gets them going," Geoff said, "gets them learning by doing."

• • • • • • • •

PERHAPS NOTHING identifies a genuine community so much as a willingness to pass on its culture to the next generation by teaching children. If that's true, then maple is the real deal. While sugarmakers may delight in the quiet woods or a long, late night of solitude beside a bubbling evaporator, such moments are fleeting. Community seems inevitable, with curious visitors, companions eager to collect sap, and rising steam that throws out the welcome mat. Come sit by the steaming evaporator, the plume telegraphs, as if it were an old-fashioned family hearth for trading stories and enjoying the comfort of company. If only by osmosis, a little sugaring knowledge and lore is imparted during such visits.

Regardless of any natural taciturnity or shyness, when it comes to sugaring, maple people grow garrulous. They are natural proselytizers, and something about the work, both process and product, makes them want to spread the gospel. There's probably no agricultural commodity that has so many hands-on educational programs for children and the general public. And because it can be as easy as a single tree and a pot on a stovetop, anyone can get involved.

There seems to be an inverse relationship between ruralism and the number of educational sugaring demonstrations in an area. As Jay Kaplan observed, such programs satisfy a genuine hunger for earthiness and a taste of farming life among suburbanites. It creates a satisfying image that combines nature and hands-on labor with colonial cauldrons and quaint Yankees on hardscrabble farms. Sandwiched between Boston and New York with isolated rural life fading to a gentrified taxidermy in many places, Connecticut is a fortunate hotbed of maple education for the general public.

New Canaan, Connecticut, is an upscale town; many of its citizens work in Manhattan. It's famous for modernist buildings, including

Philip Johnson's Glass House. On the well-groomed grounds of the New Canaan Nature Center there's an annual sugaring program, both typical and an exemplar. The sugarhouse, open on one side, is a long post-and-beam shed of board-and-batten siding with a rough, cedar-shingled roof. In the center of the shed sits an evaporator, and alongside it is an elevated platform where kids can lean against the railing and watch.

When I arrived, a young woman was explaining to a grammar school group about the Native American discovery of syrup by watching a broken branch weep sap. Wide-eyed kids sat on hay bales safely distant from the evaporator's heat as she talked about trees, boiling, and pancakes. They were transfixed, as if watching a magic act. Only a rooster crowing in the chicken coop next door broke the silence. Afterward, they all got a turn to look into the boiling evaporator pan and taste syrup on a popsicle stick.

New Canaan's program is about much more than educating school classes. Each year, individuals, groups, or families adopt the center's maple trees for seventy-five dollars apiece and "actually participate fully in this time honored tradition of New England." The program begins with an Adopt a Tree Kickoff, where participants spend approximately an hour learning about sugaring and take part in selecting and tapping their tree. Adopters are expected to collect sap one to three times weekly, depending on conditions, and take part in "in boil downs where REAL maple syrup is made." At the season's end, there's a potluck dinner where participants are encouraged to bring maple-themed foods to share, and each one gets a jug of syrup. There's also a Syrup Saturday Festival with a pancake brunch and "fun syrup related activities."

. . . .

SUGARING DEMONSTRATIONS and festivals are a staple of nature centers throughout Connecticut, each with its own style and twist. At five-hundred-acre Brooksvale Park in Hamden, a community just north of New Haven, the program is integrated into a school curriculum of environmental science and seasonal change. Up to six hundred fourth graders come to the park each year for a ninety-minute program that combines history, technological change, Indian legends, nutrition, and the science of trees and sap flow. Additional programs are held for private schools, for children with special needs, and for senior groups.

A two-foot-by-four-foot evaporator is squeezed into a converted corn crib built early in the last century and listed on the State Register of Historic Places. The site was once a dairy farm and then became the town poor farm. Here thirty to forty taps are set out on buckets, with a few on tubing for demonstration purposes. The program generally produces about ten gallons of syrup, which is sold as a park fund-raiser by a friends group.

Nature educator and sugarmaker Kirsten M. Walker is a dynamic teacher who conveys as much enthusiasm as information. With a smile and lilting voice, she invited kids from diverse backgrounds into the world of sugaring and got them participating in the learning process. Kirsten's daughter was among the first group of children to go through the program, with her mother along as a chaperone. Kirsten later volunteered, and after a few years she became the sugarmaker. I watched as she held the kids riveted around the evaporator, then had them joyfully skipping into the woods to look at trees before settling in a classroom. The program goes from tap to table. It's good, she said, for kids who like parameters—a definite beginning and end. When the final act is syrup on ice cream, it's hard not to feel good at the end.

Though she hopes kids are inspired to try sugaring at home, in thickly settled Hamden she has other goals in mind as well. It's not so much knowledge she wants to impart as it is values, a way of looking at life and the planet. Sugaring, she maintains, is a means through which the world can be experienced and explored. Kids should know that food doesn't just come from the grocery or refrigerator, but from the land. Natural foods can be better for a person's health. If children see merit in hard work, the activities will seem worthwhile, even when not glamorous or colorful. She'd like the children to understand the value of time. It takes years for a tree to grow big enough to tap, and a pint of syrup may be hours in the making. For Kirsten, sugaring is also about teaching a sense of ownership in a public park. She wants the children to realize that change need not be tied to fashion. It's cool to have outdoor experiences away from electronics.

Kirsten has an abiding faith that a new discovery, like sugaring, can change a child's world. One of the few complaints she's ever had was from a dad. He was annoyed that his child insisted upon more expensive real maple syrup after going through the program.

"Who knows where they will draw inspiration," she told me, "or where the residue of this experience will lead. When and where it translates you never know — but it can't be bad."

. . . .

A NEW MILFORD, Connecticut, sugarhouse sits behind a huge red barn along U.S. Route 202. Beyond are rolling hayfields, but there are no sugar maples at town-owned Sullivan Farm, home of Great Brook Sugarhouse. Great Brook produces a few hundred gallons from about sixteen hundred off-site trees on donated land in the next town, but such a paradox makes sense here, where sugaring is more about values than syrup. Here there's a bark-covered post with a spile and bucket just outside the sugarhouse. The hollowed inside is fitted with a plastic soda bottle whose valve can release a drip though the tap for demonstration purposes.

Sugarmaker Mark Manikin is tall and muscular, with chiseled features and glasses. He's executive director of the New Milford Youth Agency, charged with providing "positive opportunities for our community's young people . . . through Prevention, Intervention and Advocacy." The agency runs more than two dozen programs, including child care and traditional counseling.

Most of the kids sugaring, he told me, come through the court system or other government agencies or by way of friends. Some are doing community service. As a result, there's always a transient group involved in making syrup, usually about a dozen high school and college kids, along with several volunteers. Though syrup is sold to help pay for the program, the most valuable product, according to Mark, is what the kids take away long after the taste of syrup has left their tongues.

High school boys Zach and Jacob eagerly showed me around the sugarhouse and explained the workings of the three-by-ten-foot wood-fired evaporator, detailing the six-inch raised flues and Steam-Away. They traced the flow from the 1,350-gallon sap tank to the filter press and bottling process. Like some old-time Yankee ripe with years of sugaring, Zach complained that the sap was getting cloudy too early in the season, with the thermometer bound for the low sixties on that early March day. Pride of ownership radiated in the boys' smiles, although they owned nothing.

Maple helps ground people, according to Mark. The kids learn to work together and deal with the public. They get not only a sense of history, but a notion of their own relationship to the past at an annual open house that includes displays of early sugaring techniques. The intense but short and definable season "helps teach what it takes to be a leader." You have to make decisions and get people to work together. There is value to learning hands-on work and appreciating a natural process, he added.

* * * * * * * *

SOMETIMES ORGANIZATIONAL structure and formal goals aren't necessary for communal effort. "Community is where community happens," theologian Martin Buber wrote. For some reason, sugaring seems to have more than its share of spontaneous community-forming events.

A sugarmaker without earnest volunteers is unusual. I used to attract helpers of every age, from grade-schoolers to grandparents psyched to collect sap, fire the evaporator, and perform the noble and necessary role of taste tester. They would show up on weekend afternoons and even in the insomniac wee hours during the week. It's unusual to visit a sugarhouse at the season's height and not find a friend or neighbor hanging out for the camaraderie and satisfaction of working with their hands. Sometimes they prove so useful that they're rewarded with syrup or even cash. But there are times when the synergies of neighborhood effort are so tight that the operation becomes a communal possession regardless of who owns the equipment or location. The labor invested becomes a form of ownership.

In Suffield, Connecticut, not far from the Massachusetts line, Lise and Bob Howe have a sugarhouse. It's down a long dirt drive behind their house and perched at the edge of a shallow swamp. Despite its location, the operation cannot be said to belong to them alone. It's a possession of the neighborhood. During the height of the season, as many as forty people might be there offering to help, hanging out, and kibitzing. In addition to Lise and Bob, the inner circle includes Scott and Lucille Miller, who live down the road, Lise's brother Ron Guillemette, who got his start sugaring as a boy in French Canada, and his wife Kathleen. With nearly two hundred taps on buckets, there's plenty of work to go around, but a lighthearted, festive atmosphere pervades the sugarhouse. They're in it for fun.

The operation doesn't have a name, a situation perhaps unique in the maple world and evidence of the casual, homespun nature of the effort. Bob caught the sugaring bug while attending demonstrations at the Northwest Park Nature Center in Windsor, Connecticut, so it's no wonder his sugaring has become a kind of semipublic activity.

The sugarhouse itself is the embodiment of community endeavor and clever use of found materials. The evaporator sits under a central gable roof with a cupola for venting steam. There's a lean-to wood-shed on one side and a kitchen on the other. A deck out front faces the swamp, where on sunny days the crew relaxes in plastic lawn chairs. They started sugaring outside on a barrel evaporator, nicknamed "the dragon," with lasagna pans on top. Enthralled by the process, the next year they started building the sugarhouse.

An old pool deck went into part of the building's construction, and the pool's steel sidewall became the roof. Bob built the cupola in his basement with mostly scrap wood. The kitchen lean-to was added a few years later and includes a bay window that came out of the house during remodeling, along with a roof of old ductwork found at the dump. He built the cabinets from scratch, and the counter came from a cvs pharmacy that was throwing it away. The door between the kitchen and evaporator room was a dump rescue, and the aluminum door in back came from the house. The kitchen stove is a large, cast-iron Glenwood converted from coal to wood. Out back, they've constructed a five-foot-by-ten-foot "icebox" with commercial freezer insulation panels from the dump. It holds ten fifty-five-gallon barrels of sap. Their two-foot-by-six-foot Grimm evaporator with raised flues was purchased used from a seventy-two-year-old sugarmaker who, sadly, had run out of people to help him.

Bob's neighborhood and family sugarhouse may be the apex of sugaring joy. Thin, with a kind and thoughtful smile, this mechanical engineer for Hamilton Sundstrand gleefully detailed their longest continuous boil of thirty-eight hours, recalling the weariness that resulted not only in aches, but laughter. Like the best of taverns, barbershops, and small-town stores, this is a place where people gather to swap stories and make connections. Neighbors and friends run into one another and trade local news, political views, commentary on the weather, and personal concerns. On warm, sunny days they sit on the deck while the fire crackles and steam rises inside. On late nights toward the season's end, Bob said, the inner circle enjoys the otherworldly sound of peepers calling from the wetland while they lay back with a drink after collecting their frog-run sap, wondering if it might be the year's last.

Bob's gang has fun with sugar on snow, gets together for pancake breakfasts or eggs and home fries in the sugarhouse kitchen, bottles in mason jars, and sells by word of mouth. Kathleen, a redhead with short hair and glasses, cheerfully described to me her candy and taffy making. Her husband makes maple cream.

On a sunny Sunday afternoon the place was alive with smiling faces and laughter. Bob stood on the deck looking out at the half-thawed swamp whose opaque coating of ice reminded me of a cataract-occluded eye. He likes the atmosphere of an oncoming season, he said, because as sap begins to rise in the trees so does his own energy level, anticipating the happy labor ahead. "At last I know spring is coming, and sugaring makes me hyperaware of changes in nature." He smiled. "Best of all, it makes the end of winter go by quickly."

* * * * * * * *

MUCH IS MADE OF sugarmakers as a community or extended family, but few operations bring that notion into as sharp relief as Russ and Debbie Jordan's SlapHappy's Sap Shack in Cummington, Massachusetts. Russ's family has lived on this rolling ground between the Connecticut River and the Berkshires since the mid-eighteenth century. His grandfather sugared nearby during the 1920s and 1930s. A facilities and property manager, Russ is talented with his hands and decided that sugaring would be a good way to spend time with his eldest son. The two began gathering equipment and knowledge, but before they could start making syrup Josh became ill. In 2002, he died of leukemia at age twelve.

It wasn't until 2009, after Russ moved into a new home with his wife Debbie, that he felt up to sugaring again. He made a gallon using a stockpot over a makeshift fire pit in their driveway. As he stood by his rig on a rainy day, umbrella in one hand and a beer in the other, Debbie called to him from the house. "Are you having fun?" she asked. "This is real living," he replied cheerfully. He was hooked.

By 2011, Russ had built a twelve-by-twelve sugarhouse and made eight gallons from fifty taps on a nineteen-by-forty-eight-inch flat-bottom pan. They had more than they could use or give to family and friends. Debbie suggested they sell some of it, and Russ decided to donate the gross to the American Cancer Society in memory of Josh and in honor of Debbie. She's a breast cancer survivor who had been diagnosed shortly after the two began courting. The following year they made eleven gallons and again donated all the receipts, absorbing the expenses for equipment, jugs, and everything else out of their own pockets.

To Russ's surprise, a Saturday mail delivery in 2013 brought a letter from Bradley Gillilan at Leader Evaporator. Debbie had written to the company requesting a discounted two-foot-by-six-foot evaporator to help them in their "pursuit for a cure." She described Russ as someone whose "heart is all giving" and detailed his courage in marrying someone with cancer so soon after losing his son. "He is a very humble man and I am in awe of him," her letter read. "He is my hero."

Reading Bradley's positive response to Debbie's letter brought Russ to tears. The company not only offered them an evaporator for free, but help setting it up and showing them how to operate it efficiently. In exchange, all Leader wanted was to feature them in its catalog and get periodic updates with photos. "It is easy during these times to lose sight of what the root of maple is all about," wrote Leader president Gary Gaudette in the spring/summer 2014 Leader catalog. "At the heart of making maple syrup is time spent with family and friends."

There's "hardly a family that hasn't been affected by cancer," Bruce Gillilan told me as we sat in his Fletcher, Vermont, sugarhouse on a warm June day. He choked up and wiped away some incipient tears as we talked. "We get a lot of charitable solicitations, and we try to help where we can, but we've never given away an evaporator. Debbie's letter hit us in the gut. Bradley saw it first and brought it to Gary, who told him to do what he thought was right." Cancer *did* hit most every family, I thought, thinking of my own family as I also wiped away a few tears.

I picked up the Leader catalog bearing a pink ribbon on its cover while my wife Mary and I were at the hall of fame induction ceremony in Croghan. I skimmed the unusual story of SlapHappy's Sap Shack, but being almost done with my work on this book didn't think I'd include it. On our long drive back from New York, we stopped for dinner at the New Boston Inn in Sandisfield, Massachusetts, just forty-five minutes from home. Sitting in the dimly lit and cozy taproom that has served travelers since colonial times, we struck up a conversation with some folks at the bar, including a friend of Russ and Debbie's who told us their tale, gave me Russ's contact information, and then a taste of his own backyard syrup. First hearing about Slap-Happy's twice in a single day by such diverse means and hundreds of miles apart was a coincidence too strong to ignore. "It was meant to be," Mary whispered to me on the way home. I called the next day, and before the week was out I was sitting with Russ and Debbie, sipping coffee at a table in the back of their sugarhouse.

The loving sweetness between them was evident as they recounted their story, sometimes punctuated by tears when recalling Josh's painful cancer ordeal and Debbie's fight for survival through hospitals and doctors, procedures and medications. I felt welcomed into their world, a sudden old friend. They were overwhelmed with Leader's generosity, including the time and friendship Bradley offered when setting up.

"What once took twelve to fourteen hours to boil now takes a little over three," said Russ, a tall man with a goatee and glasses whose full head of hair grew back after he shaved it in sympathy with his son. They've expanded to 223 taps, 156 of which are on gravity tubing. They made forty-one gallons of syrup in 2014, and have collected $1,000 so far, Debbie said proudly. A medical facility nurse, she has blue eyes that speak with sincerity, a soft voice, and an amiable smile. I bought a jug of syrup and added to their total.

The sugarhouse is a rustic board-and-batten structure to which Russ has added an addition to accommodate the new evaporator. He's overwhelmed at the outpouring of support they've received. On hearing their story, Daryl Sheets, a sugarmaker from Meadville, Pennsylvania, who builds filter presses, donated a machine. Marcland Instruments of Schroon Lake, New York, a small company that makes automatic draw-off valves, gave them one for cost. They may get a donated vacuum pump.

Like Russ's reason for boiling, the sugarhouse is deeply personal. The walls and shelves are filled with his life's enthusiasms—Tonka toys (some from his boyhood), lanterns, hubcaps (including one from a Model T Ford), and objects collected from outdoors like rocks, birds' nests, and a papery white-faced hornets' nest.

The cause may be of the utmost gravity, but Russ and Debbie approach sugaring with a deep reservoir of joy. Come next season, I'll be back to share a boil with them.

· · · · · · ·

IT'S HARD to imagine a sugaring operation that doesn't involve family and friends. Although you'd think that the biggest, technology-heavy ones would be more corporate and less communal, to some extent the opposite is true.

At 1.2 million, Maine's Somerset County has more maple taps than any other in the country. With four thousand square miles, it's almost 25 percent larger than Delaware and Rhode Island combined, but so sparsely settled it has only thirteen people per square mile. Situated in the west-central part of the state, it shares a long boundary with Quebec province along the Southwest Branch of the St. John River. Much of the area is in unincorporated townships comprising vast forest tracts once owned by large paper companies and now under the aegis of timber investment management organizations that oversee the land for institutional investors.

In Somerset County, some folks boast, you're more likely to encounter moose or bear than human beings. It's an area of active timber harvesting where dinosaur-like machines can snap mature trees as easily as hand clippers cut a garden rose. The region is laced with rough woods roads, providing access for tree cutting, that are impassable by conventional vehicles. Unpaved, washboarded, and potholed arterial routes enable heavily laden logging trucks lacking weight limits to barrel at frightful speeds in clouds of dust. Visitors can encounter hazardous travel due to rough surfaces, animals, fallen trees, and oncoming trucks.

Sugaring operations are large, about thirty thousand taps on average, with some in excess of eighty thousand. The vast majority of Maine syrup is produced in this region, remote from tourists and retail outlets, which means nearly all of it is sold in bulk. Most of the sugarhouses are run by French Canadians from nearby towns in Quebec like Saint-Zacharie, Sainte-Aurélie, Sainte-Justine, and Saint-Cyprien. Typically multigenerational family businesses, they are maple islands in an industrial forest dominated by paper and wood-products concerns. Isolated, generating their own electricity, and coping with border restrictions, some of these families have yet persevered for a century.

Several Octobers ago, I visited the region with a busload of sugarmakers from around the country and Canada, courtesy of the Maine Maple Producers Association, which had hosted the North American Maple Syrup Council meeting that year. We spent three days on the dusty, bone-rattling Golden Road, the grand trunk of logging access, and various lesser forest highways. There's a distinct rhythm to riding these roads, with the rattle and bounce of rough surfaces and the slush of mud. I heard the ping of stones against the vehicle's frame and sometimes the clank of a large rock. When a speeding logging truck went past, its wake of sand and dirt hitting the bus sounded like sleet.

Deep in thick woods, the road felt like a canal between the trees. Bare hardwoods glistened in thin white light among dark pockets of fir and spruce standing like folded umbrellas. Towering pines loomed over the forest like sylvan princes. Occasionally, light poured into the bus as we passed desultory swamps, amoeba-shaped lakes, or a logging clearing.

The bus filled with sugarmaker chitchat about the impact of severe summer thunderstorms on sap sugar content and volume. There was debate over climate change, fretting about the Asian long-horned beetle, and strong opinions about the effect of ro on flavor. A small group in back got into a heated argument over wood versus oil-fired evaporators. Most in Somerset are fueled by oil, and someone who had been here during the season said that tank trucks running along the roads are the dominant sound from mid-March to mid-April.

In this part of the world, maple facilities are called "sugar camps." Most include not only space for the evaporator, storage, and processing, but also living quarters for the families that spend a few months of each year here. Perhaps because they typically live in the same building in which they make syrup, the inhabitants are particularly meticulous. "These sugarhouses are spotless," remarked a sugarmaker from the Midwest when we were making our way home. "No wonder they make good syrup."

Traveling Baker Lake Road, we passed a relatively flat area where medium-size hardwoods dominated and were strung with the familiar sight of soft blue tubing. Soon we had arrived at the sugar camp of Guy Rodrigue, a little over four miles from the Canadian border. The sugarhouse was a long, corrugated steel building with a similar material for the roof. It was typical for the area except for the bright aqua doors. The sugarmakers, including Guy and his son Michael, were all Francophones, and their English was heavily accented. Regardless, their pride in the operation and excitement at entertaining far-off visitors were clear in any language. Their thirty-six thousand taps were handled by three RO machines, a seven-thousand-gallon sap tank, and a gleaming evaporator that could produce forty-five gallons of syrup an hour on thirty gallons of oil. April first had been their biggest day ever, with forty-two drums of syrup made in twenty-four hours.

At Rheaume et Bernard Rodrigue not far away, we were treated to lunch at long tables set up in the kitchen and living room, both fitted with light-colored paneling. Though the building was another long, gable-roofed steel structure with gleaming stacks within which syrup was made, the living quarters inside were warm and cozy, well lit, with comfortable furniture that belied the industrial exterior. Nearby were separate sheds for pumps, electric generators, and storage. Three generations fed us, answered questions, and showed off the equipment at this seventy-seven-thousand-tap operation. They seemed to take genuine joy in our presence, as if we were long-lost family. Out in the middle of nowhere, we feasted on fresh-baked bread, meatball and potato stew, pork pie, baked beans with maple, and bacon and maple pie for dessert. They'd even saved a large pan of snow from a recent storm and, pouring hot syrup on it, gave us popsicle sticks with which to dig at the taffy-like confection.

At some of the camps, living quarters were quite elaborate. Bernard Jolin's metal sugarhouse with its bright-red roof included an elegant living area featuring fine ceramic tile and beautiful woodwork. Bernard's wife Anny spends the season with him, and their three children—Albert, Melodie, and Zachary—have the run of the place. Bernard, a relatively young man, told us that sugaring had become his passion as a boy, and buying the sugarbush in 1991 fulfilled his longtime dream. He had worked hard to grow it from fifty-seven hundred taps to twenty thousand and hoped for more.

Sugaring was a way for Bernard's family to keep close together, at least for part of the year. He took great pleasure in seeing his kids enjoy the adventure of life in the woods combined with the alternating quiet and frenetic activity of maple production. He loved being here from snowpack to leaf-out, watching the world come alive. "Chez moi, le printemps est toujours un moment très attendu—to me it is a pleasure to see the spring coming up," he translated.

At the camp of Jinny Lamontague and Odette Gilbert, set in a low spot surrounded by trees strung with tubing, wide-eyed children marveled at the bus. Built by Jinny's grandfather in 1907 with an ax and other hand tools, the wooden sugarhouse is an ancient-looking structure with a metal roof, tall shining stack, and traditional cupola. It's dimly lit and drafty, with a decided lean that makes it seem as if it might collapse in a heavy snow. When it was built, wooden buckets were placed on the snow below tapholes, and horses carried sap to the sugarhouse. The gleaming oil-fired evaporator takes up almost the entire interior and seems to draw all the light to its stainless pans.

We walked out and over to the tight clapboard cabin where the family lived. Jinny learned everything from his parents, he told us as the kids darted through the crowd, chasing each other. Though the old sugarhouse was filled with memories, he said he was committed to modernization. "It will be the only way to survive and give something to the children."

In the sugaring world, unlike most businesses, bigger doesn't mean impersonal, and friendly is not synonymous with low-tech. Perhaps it's because sugaring is more than a business. It's a way of life, a means of knowing the world, part of a person's very identity. Pride of place and labor are inextricably fused.

. . . .

THE POWER OF maple to draw people together and create community is as simple, yet as alchemical, as the transformation of sap to syrup. No doubt sugaring season helped Native Americans, the original sugarmakers, with both nutritional and social sustenance. Thus, it should come as no surprise that the fabulously wealthy Mashantucket Pequot tribe of southeastern Connecticut, owners of one of the world's largest casinos, first tried sugaring as a way of reestablishing its community and drawing people back to the reservation.

Sugaring was "one of the first economic endeavors in the 1970s that pulled the community together and was a symbol of unity," reads a card in the tribe's museum gift shop, describing a commemorative blanket depicting the sugarhouse and other tribal icons. An exhibit in the museum includes a photograph of the simple sugarhouse with cupola and weathered vertical siding, a far cry from the glitz of the palatial structures on the reservation today. Next to the photograph are a couple of sample syrup jugs that show a nostalgic forest scene inked in red. "Because there were so many maple trees on the reservation," reads a narrative below the photo, "maple sugaring seemed like a natural business prospect. Many tribal members, including children, participated in the project, carrying buckets of sap from the trees to the 'sugar shack,' where the sap was boiled into syrup. Despite the hard work, tribal members remember the festive atmosphere during the maple sugar project and eating delicious hot dogs boiled in sap."

Although making syrup fell by the wayside upon the development of the casino, in a few sentences here is the essence of sugaring described by descendants of the people who started it all. Boiled down to its basics, it amounts to maple trees, joint effort, hard work, and fun.

Maple Syrup Pie

Yield: One 9-inch pie

INGREDIENTS
2 ¼ cups maple syrup
¾ cup light cream
¼ cup all-purpose flour
4 eggs
1 cup walnuts (optional)
9-inch unbaked pie shell

DIRECTIONS
1. Preheat oven to 375°F.
2. In a bowl, whisk together the maple syrup, light cream, flour, and eggs until blended. Stir in the nuts, if desired.
3. Pour the mixture into the crust.
4. Bake in a 375°F oven for 10 minutes; reduce the heat to 350° and continue baking for an additional 30−35 minutes or until set. Let cool on rack.

Recipe by Betsey Dalton

Quick Maple Fudge

Yield: 9-inch square pan makes nine 3-inch squares

INGREDIENTS
12 ounces confectioners' sugar
8 ounces granulated maple sugar
¼ cup milk
½ cup butter
14 full-size marshmallows
¾ cup chopped nuts
1 teaspoon vanilla extract

DIRECTIONS

1. Place all ingredients except vanilla into a microwave-safe bowl. Microwave on high for about four minutes, until all ingredients are melted. Time depends on the microwave.

2. Add the vanilla extract and stir well to combine. Pour into containers to set and cool.

Fresh confectioners' sugar and marshmallows are a must for good results with this recipe!

Recipe by Rob and Jean Lamothe

Food for Thought

THOUGH I'VE NEVER tried a case, I'm a lawyer by trade. Like many in the profession, I've experienced at least fleeting moments when I've desired to be a judge, the seeming apex of the legal world. With a career path that rarely took me into a courtroom, such fantasies never lasted long. But on a sunny September afternoon in 2002 I found myself elevated to the bench with a brief brevet appointment on the occasion of the twenty-fifth anniversary of the Maple Syrup Producers Association of Connecticut, of which I was a director.

The sun was strong, the air cool, and the sky punctuated by large cumulus clouds at Northwest Park in Windsor, where the association's longtime secretary, Chuck Drake, has for many years run a small educational sugaring operation in an old shed once part of a tobacco farm. Completely to my surprise, I was asked to judge a pie-baking contest. Among the entries were maple apple and maple pecan pies, as well as a maple cream pie and a maple cheesecake. While the cheesecake might not technically be a pie, it looked the part in a Pyrex baking dish. Pie is one of my favorite foods, and when the calendar rolls around to my birthday you can forget cake. Bring me pie.

Of course, I was delighted at the honor, and fell to my task with equal parts boyish joy and judicial gravitas. Complete with an apron as my badge of office, I carefully cut myself a slice of the seven pies arrayed on a picnic table and began carefully to taste. It was hard not to down them with gusto, but to instead slowly nibble and savor in careful evaluation. The task was more difficult than I had imagined, and like a wine taster I kept comparative notes on a pad. I evaluated flavor, of course; but texture, appearance, and originality counted as well. I considered the overall pie, the intensity of maple flavor, and the texture and taste of the crust. I also had to fight against my natural affinity and potential bias for pecan pie, a dish I've made many times over the years.

Pie tasting was the sweetest job I've ever had. Some contestants won prizes, others did not, but the judge was always a winner, consuming as much of the delicious confections as he wanted. After the contest was over everyone had dessert, and not a slice remained to take home.

* * * * * * *

ABOVE ALL, maple syrup is a food. This may seem obvious, but both sugarmakers and the public often forget, sometimes treating it like a rare elixir, magical potion, the essence of a season and way of life, an iconic symbol. Though we take maple syrup into our bodies and it helps sustain us, it is not consumed for its own sake like an apple, egg, or steak. Rather, it's a food that enlivens other foods. Like a spice, it's an additive to something else. This quality creates endless opportunities for its use, but also requires some effort and creativity. The myriad ways one can use a piece of cheese or a head of lettuce in the kitchen are fairly obvious, but "syrup" is a word that to most Americans says only one thing: pancakes.

Despite this disadvantage, maple syrup resides in that pantheon of foods revered for their special qualities. Maybe it's the simplicity or all-natural aspect, but maple syrup is not only edible — it's a food you can believe in. It may be among the last wild foods. Although a few planted maples are tapped, sap is harvested almost totally from forests. "We are what we eat," writes Robin Wall Kimmerer, "and with every golden spoonful maple carbon becomes human carbon. My ninety-six-year-old grandma likes to take a pure spoonful once in a while, when she's feeling low. She calls it vitamin M."

If any proof is required of maple syrup's versatility enhancing the flavor of other foods, all one needs do is walk into any gift shop that features maple products, a sugarhouse with a sales counter, or thumb through a maple-themed catalog to see a wide selection of cookbooks. Among the many titles are *Simply Maple*; *Cooking with Maple Syrup*; *Dishing Up Vermont*; *A Taste of Maple*; *Just Naturally Sweet*; *Very Maple Syrup*; *The Vermont Maple Festival Blue Ribbon Recipes*; *New Hampshire Maple Recipes*; and *High Acres Maple Syrup Cookbook*. The recipes that appear in these volumes are wide-ranging and clever. They're not just about breakfast or dessert but include maple-barbecued pork ribs, maple-oatmeal bread, maple roast chicken, maple syrup and balsamic vinegar, maple teriyaki salmon, baked eggs in maple toast caps, maple-cranberry relish, corned beef brisket braised with maple and bourbon, maple broiled scallops, maple whiskey sours, and red cabbage braised with maple syrup.

Maple syrup is a surprisingly multipurpose additive to just about any kind of cooking. The possibilities are limited only by the imaginations of restaurant chefs, foodies, and home kitchen cooks. But the image of syrup on pancakes is so fixed in the public mind that it's almost a hindrance to wider use of the golden liquid. No doubt, with proper marketing maple could become the go-to sweetener in many recipes.

I often ask sugarmakers about their favorite maple foods. Sometimes they hesitate because there is typically more than one, and picking among them would be like choosing a favorite child. Many are sweets also beloved by the general public. Their choices are almost never casual, and sometimes they become almost rhapsodic in their descriptions, as if recalling tastes, smells, and textures embedded deep in heartfelt memory.

Lyle Merrifield licked his lips on mentioning maple-glazed scallops wrapped in bacon. Business-minded Bruce Bascom got a little misty, his face softening as he recalled the maple pecan pie his mom used to make. The elderly Bolduc brothers smiled when they told me that in days past they kept a brandy bottle by the evaporator to mix with fresh, unfiltered syrup right from the pan. Burr Morse's eyes lit as he recalled the delicious, cooling simplicity of first-run fancy syrup over vanilla ice cream. But then he hesitated, got a far-off look that momentarily took him away from me and the steaming evaporator. He seemed to snap back suddenly and described in warm, careful detail the biscuits with maple syrup sauce he enjoyed at his grandparents' kitchen table. I could almost see him reaching back in time and tasting them.

Maple is a changeling food — chameleonlike, protean. Until almost the twentieth century, with the advent of better transportation, refrigeration, and canning techniques, practically all sap became solid sugar. Yet with the exception of candy, solid maple sugar is virtually unknown to consumers today. In fact, it has almost disappeared from the market, despite a recent revival in granulated form, a product akin to how we typically encounter cane sugar, though coarser and more flavorful.

As James Dina points out, Native Americans lacked bottles with screw tops, making transporting syrup difficult. Spills that wasted such a tediously created product (and which could make a sticky mess) were to be avoided. European colonists generally used molasses as their sticky liquid sweetener and, following what they learned from the natives, used maple in its solid block form, carving off chips as needed. Knowledge of this history, combined with savvy Yankee insight and a lot of time spent in the woods and beside the evaporator, has led sugarmakers to create new ways to use maple and engage the public taste in innovative flavor combinations.

· · · · · · · ·

SUGARMAKERS HAVE a strong, burly, outdoorsman image akin to the iconic woodsy perception of their product. You don't think of them as spending much time in the kitchen, and hardly donning an apron and working with measuring cups, loaf pans, cookie sheets, and turkey basters. But finding new products and improving on existing ones are key to maximizing the value per ounce of syrup, so many sugarmakers quietly spend long hours experimenting. Some work in home kitchens, perhaps while preparing breakfast or dinner, and use their families as guinea pigs. Others have kitchens in their sugarhouses that are more like laboratories with gleaming tile and stainless-steel surfaces, commercial ovens and stoves. It's all part of the effort to get beyond pancakes, waffles, and the occasional dessert, a pursuit that's become more critical in recent years with the U.S. industry expanding at a rate of 10 percent annually and needing to find new outlets for the additional product.

Everyone from academic scientists to backyard sugarmakers wants to come up with the next irresistible snack food or confection that will become a taste sensation. Many of them like to tinker with traditional maple goodies, like nuts, to get some distinctive flavor or texture that will distinguish their product from the rest.

Breakfast at Davenport Maple Farm

Though competition from other edibles and increased syrup supplies have sharpened the need in recent years, tinkering with maple-flavored foods is not new. Russ Davenport recalls experimenting with cranberries decades ago. A relative on Cape Cod sent him a thousand pounds of the tart red fruits, and he thought that sweetening them with maple sugar might turn them into a snack you could just pop in your mouth. He tried all sorts of temperatures, sugar densities, and other formulas, but sugar would not stick on the berries. Experiment after experiment went awry, and he felt deep frustration over something that seemed so easy. Almost by accident, he found that if he broke the skin and dried the berries they would take the sugar. He invented a machine that would split them open, and then he put the berries in a fruit drier. Russ found the maple cranberries delicious, but they never became a big seller. Although he had them patented as "crannies," at renewal time he let the patent expire as not worth the cost.

The range of products made or sold by even small and medium-size operations is remarkable. Lyle Merrifield offers granulated maple sugar, maple-coated nuts, smoked maple cheese, maple cream, and maple butter. He can't keep maple candy in stock very long, it's so popular. Not many producers bother with maple cotton candy because they see it having specialized appeal and worry about a short shelf life relative to other products, but Lyle gets a charge out of watching the wide eyes of children light up when they take a bite of the woolly, tan-colored treat.

Rob Lamothe and his wife Jean are experimenters who seem to work with the determination and eager delight of movie mad scientists. As the sugarhouse has expanded over the years to include an ell with a country store, so has the size of the kitchen. It's spacious, with stainless-steel ovens and refrigerators and a long row of cookbooks. They sell many different maple products, and all are made on premises from formulas developed as they tinkered in the kitchen. Their line features maple coffee and applesauce, maple spice rub for meats, maple almonds, cashews, peanuts, kettle corn, apple jam, mustard, barbecue sauce, candy, cookie mixes, and fudge, and maple pepper.

Every year or so they try to come up with a new product because it sparks their customers, renewing their interest in all things maple. A more recent addition to their line is barbecue sauce, which took quite a bit of trial and error to get right. While they will gladly share their general sugaring knowledge with anyone listening, the Lamothes, like most sugarmakers, consider their food recipes proprietary and keep them locked in a safe.

Among their biggest sellers are maple-coated nuts, so they're always looking for new varieties to offer. You'd think that walnuts would be a natural, and so did they. Rob and Jean tried various formulas over four years of experimentation with the temperature, grade, and amount of syrup used, as well as cooling and packing techniques. Unfortunately, the finished product had a short shelf life and often turned rancid because, they concluded, there was a lot of natural moisture in the walnuts. They remain determined to solve the problem, and Rob effervesces with ideas. Meanwhile, excitement over other foods has captured their attention for a while.

More often than not, long hours in the kitchen pay off. Working with scientists at Cornell, Rob built his own maple-cream machine. Maple cream, also called maple butter, is a spread like hummus or peanut butter. Unfortunately, it tends to separate over time. Although this doesn't affect flavor, it makes it look unappetizing. Rob's machine included the unusual feature of directly filling containers, thereby reducing air pockets, which contribute to product instability. Combined with his and Jean's adjustments of temperature, syrup grade, use of invertase (a confectionary enzyme that breaks down sugar), and other techniques, the machine enabled them to create a highly shelf-stable and attractive product that allowed production of larger batches that were also more acceptable to consumers.

Even smaller producers like Tom Buck find the lure of maple-flavored foods irresistible. It's not just about the added revenue, but the diversity of activity, family engagement, and the deepening of their journey into the maple world. Tom makes candy meticulously and tediously by hand in rubbery molds, as do many sugarmakers. He produces maple cream and granulated sugar, and is on the verge of getting into maple cotton candy. He's found a maple cookie recipe he likes. Though it never proved a big seller, at one time he made maple jelly, a versatile product used for everything from spreading on toast to a dipping sauce for sliced meat.

Tom effervesced as he spoke about the possibilities, like an old-time elixir salesman hawking a panacea. His wife Lois makes and sells maple kettle corn at summer fairs, and he's delighted to have her involved in sugaring. They are contemplating buying a concession trailer where they could also make maple-cream-covered cider doughnuts. He flashed his warm, gap-toothed smile and told me about his plans for making nut brittle, mustard, and salad dressings. He shrugged. "I'll need a commercial kitchen at least as big as my sugarhouse to do it all."

• • • • • • •

THE SEARCH FOR more maple products is not just a matter of finding an outlet for a currently expanding industry. It's also about potential. Less than 1 percent of tappable U.S. trees are in syrup production. Consumption is less than three ounces per capita, and only twice that in Canada, while on the rest of the globe it's barely detectable, according to Mike Farrell. If even a fraction of that prospective syrup production is to become reality, the maple world not only must go further than pancakes, but also has to think outside the syrup jug, with maple as an ingredient in new products that will absorb additional production. As a result, experimenting with new maple-flavored foods has gone beyond the sugarhouse. Agricultural educators and extension agents like Stephen Childs, a New York State maple specialist in Cornell's cooperative extension, are working feverishly to develop and promote new items like maple marshmallows, soda, and lollipops.

Not only are new uses of maple being developed outside the sugarhouse—they are happening beyond the world of sugaring, with beverage makers leading innovation in recent years. The Vermont Sweetwater Bottling Company is a small, family-run soda works started in the 1990s when brothers Bob and Rich Munch were drinking maple sap while doing some backyard sugaring and decided that a little added carbonation would make a tasty beverage. They experimented for a while, finally hitting on a good formula. Today, their Vermont Maple Seltzer is produced in an old dairy barn on a dirt road. Some of the bottling equipment dates to the 1940s. The seltzer is made with sap containing 3.5 percent sugar in a patented process involving pasteurization and carbonation. It is clear and has a slightly sweet but refreshing maple flavor.

A few years later, the brothers developed Vermont Maple Soda, sweetened only with an ounce of maple syrup per twelve-ounce bottle. The soda is naturally caramel colored and has a distinct maple flavor with toasted marshmallow and toffee accents. They remain a tiny player in the beverage industry, producing about four thousand cases of maple drinks per year, as well as seven other soda flavors. So far, none of the big multinational companies appear to have taken notice. But theirs is potentially a breakthrough product when one considers that the average American drinks close to forty-five gallons of soda a year.

Brewers have been experimenting with maple, especially for seasonal products, and there are now maple ales and porters and sap beers. At first they were offered only on tap in brewpubs and selected taverns, but now they are often widely bottled. Among the more interesting brews I've sampled are Samuel Adams Maple Pecan Porter made with Vermont maple syrup by the Boston Beer Company, and Harpoon Brewery's Catamount Maple Wheat Ale, which was made in a 2012 limited edition with Vermont maple syrup at their Vermont brewery. The taste of maple wasn't very strong, but it added a delicate sweetness and body. In Delaware, Dogfish Head Craft Brewery uses maple syrup from western Massachusetts to make its high-alcohol Immort Ale, which it describes as "vast in character, luscious and complex. Pour it over pancakes." Oregon's Rogue Ales brews Voodoo Bacon Maple Ale, described as having "a rich amber color with a big aroma of sweet maple balanced by the spicy flavor of smoked bacon." The company suggests dessert, doughnuts, and pork as food pairings.

Distillers have also discovered syrup, and it can be found in liqueurs and whiskies. Boyden Valley Winery, a neatly kept farm run by three generations and located in a bucolic area of Cambridge, Vermont, makes a Vermont Ice Maple Cream Liqueur from its own syrup, apple brandy from local apples, and cream. It's like a maple milkshake, smooth and rich. Saxtons River Distillery, located in a rectangular steel building just north of Brattleboro, Vermont, produces Sapling Maple Liqueur with one-third dark syrup. It also makes maple-flavored rye and bourbon products containing 25 percent syrup. All are incredibly smooth, with the maple flavor amped by the power of whiskey. Owner Christian Stromberg said he got the idea from the honey liqueur made by his Lithuanian family, who fled czarist Russia in 1906.

First marketed in 2006, Cabin Fever Maple Flavored Whiskey, made with dark syrup, is three years old and eighty proof. According to the product website, Rob Robillard got started by building a still from two welded-together lobster cooking pots in his family's New Hampshire garage. It's described as being "a delicate blend of leathery oak and maple that comes together in harmony." Crown Royal, which gets its flavor from aging in maple-seared barrels, and Jim Beam are also among the companies now marketing maple-flavored whiskies. The flavor in nationally distributed products is artificial, Mike Farrell discovered after speaking with people at these businesses.

Wine is yet another beverage opportunity for maple syrup. Boyden Valley makes a Vermont Maple Wine out of Northern Spy apples and syrup. The mix of tart and sweet is intriguing. Some maple wine has come onto the market in the form of mead, or honey wine. Mead is an ancient beverage dating back thousands of years and may be considered the ancestor of all alcoholic drinks. The Sap House Meadery, founded in 2010 in Center Ossipee, New Hampshire, has created an award-winning mead using maple syrup. The winery claims that the beverage will bring to mind "caramel, toffee, apples and of course maple syrup." They also use maple syrup in their Hopped Blueberry and Cranberry Sage Mead.

• • • • • • • •

PARADOXICALLY, at the same time maple is seeing growth in snack food, soda, and alcoholic beverage markets, it also is gaining cachet as a health food. Of course, syrup has always been touted as a pure, natural product free of additives, preservatives, and artificial ingredients. It's long been a standard of health food outlets and co-ops, favored by those seeking what's organic and unrefined. But maple syrup may be undergoing a revival as a new super-food, a miracle sweetener, even.

Calling maple syrup "the only commercial product in our diet that comes from a plant's sap," Navindra Seeram, an assistant professor of biomedical and pharmaceutical sciences at the University of Rhode Island's College of Pharmacy, has found over fifty compounds in maple syrup that may be beneficial to human health, including some that are newly discovered. Many are antioxidants that act as anti-inflammatory agents. According to Seeram, syrup also contains polyphenols that inhibit enzymes involved with conversion of carbohydrates to sugar and thus may have some antidiabetic properties that could inhibit type 2 diabetes. He's also found abscisic acid, a compound believed to stimulate the pancreas to release insulin.

A self-characterized "plant natural product chemist," Dr. Seeram described sap on National Public Radio's *Science Friday* program as "the tree's lifeblood . . . because it's taking nutrients from the roots all the way to the leaves." The tree "is producing these phytochemicals, and it's getting into the sap and then ending up in the syrup, because you're really concentrating it down." Many elements of this polyphenol cocktail of compounds have well-documented health benefits already publicized in berries, tea, red wine, and flaxseed. While more work needs to be done to determine whether these chemicals exist in beneficial concentrations, "we do know that the sheer quantity and variety of identified compounds with documented health benefits qualifies maple syrup as a champion food," according to a 2011

Federation of Quebec Maple Syrup Producers' press release quoting Dr. Seeram.

Although the research is being done in New England, it's funded by the big syrup cartel north of the border. "They would have a vested interest," *Science Friday* host Ira Flatow noted in his interview, "but it doesn't mean that you haven't found what you found." Dr. Seeram didn't hesitate. "No," he said, "research is research."

While Dr. Seeram's work has grabbed some headlines in the ever-competitive arena of healthful foods, maple syrup has long been known to contain a variety of valuable nutrients, and increasingly visitors find colorful nutrition charts tacked to the walls of sugarhouses and retail outlets. Maple syrup is rich in minerals, especially calcium, potassium, manganese, magnesium, phosphorus, and iron. Among vitamins essential to health, maple syrup includes vitamin B2 (riboflavin), B5 (pantothenic acid), B6 (pyridoxine), B1 (niacin), and folic acid.

Nutrient comparisons with corn syrup—a substance that some have fingered as empty calories primarily responsible for the nation's obesity epidemic—are particularly striking. Maple syrup has fewer calories and less sugar per unit. It contains overwhelmingly more manganese, riboflavin, zinc, magnesium, calcium, and potassium. Ubiquitous in our diet, corn syrup is found in potato chips, soda, ketchup, barbecue sauces, and salad dressings. It's also the only sweetener in table syrups like Log Cabin and Aunt Jemima.

• • • • • • •

PHYSICAL FITNESS enthusiasts are increasingly advocating use of maple syrup before, during, and after workouts. "Before you hit the gym," recommends a 2013 article at Stack.com, a website devoted to athletic training, "try incorporating maple syrup into your pre-workout snack"; the syrup is cited for its ability to deliver carbs with "anti-inflammatory compounds that help protect cells from oxidative damage." The article also maintained that an "all natural maple sports drink is designed to keep up stamina during training sessions and keep up electrolyte levels." For getting "valuable minerals" back after a tough workout, like manganese and zinc, a "fruity maple recovery shake is recommended."

Physical culture self-help websites like registered dietitian Martha McKittrick's citygirlbites.com, have personal "fit maple" tips like maple syrup mixed into oatmeal or a yogurt/banana shake. She touts the antioxidant compounds and "beneficial vitamins and minerals" in this "all-natural energy booster that may surprise you." A "fan of natural versus processed foods," she "readily agreed to be a spokesperson for the Fit Maple Campaign" of the Quebec federation.

The leading health fad involving maple syrup is the Master Cleanse, also known as the Maple Syrup Detox Diet. It was developed by naturopath Stanley Burroughs in the 1940s and made widely known by his 1970s book *Healing for the Age of Enlightenment*, the bible for both the recipe and the philosophical underpinnings of the program. Burroughs believed in the body's natural healing capabilities when given the proper diet and other treatments. Some take umbrage at the term "diet" because they look at the process as principally valuable for cleansing the body of toxins, a means of changing lifestyle, and a way of turning away from addictions like tobacco, junk food, and alcohol.

Claims have been made that the program scrubs clean the digestive tract and kidneys, rids waste in the muscles and joints, relieves stress, and creates a healthier bloodstream. Some people insist that it can prevent or control flu, asthma, sinus issues, and hay fever. Others find the diet an extreme fad whose cleansing claims have no basis and can have long-term negative health effects, such as loss of muscle mass. Still, it remains attractive to some people as a way to lose as much as a pound per day. In 2006, "the cleanse" got a big boost when actress and singer Beyoncé Knowles used it to quickly lose twenty pounds for her role in the film *Dream Girls.*

Dieters on the Master Cleanse drink a mixture consisting of two tablespoons of organic lemon juice, two tablespoon of organic-grade B (now called "very dark with strong taste") maple syrup, a tenth of a teaspoon of ground cayenne pepper, and ten ounces of filtered water six to a dozen times a day. Some have the expectation of a "whole new you" in ten days, as Raylen Sterling, publisher of the *Master Cleanse Secrets* newsletter put it. "It restores your body to its normal healthy state," she claims, and eliminates pounds of putrid waste for good.

As I walked through Bruce Bascom's storehouse stacked with syrup drums on one of my visits, I asked him if there were any trends in regard to syrup grades. "Lots more demand for dark syrup since that lemonade and maple diet caught fire," he said. "Does that really work?" I asked, not familiar with the program at the time. He shrugged. "Whether it does or not, it's good for business," he replied laconically.

· · · · · · ·

AS A SHELF-STABLE product that has engendered few problems because of its high sugar content, maple syrup wasn't subject to much government regulatory scrutiny in the past. Because it was boiled, it was considered low risk for contaminating organisms. But the days of filtering sap through an old sock, boiling in a sugarhouse storing pesticides for the orchard, or making candy in your home kitchen and selling what the family doesn't eat are fading, if not gone.

With increasing use of maple syrup as an additive in other foods and rising consciousness of its health value, there is more public interest in how maple syrup is made. This has brought increased scrutiny of processing, a new emphasis on sanitation, and more government food-safety regulation. Such public and bureaucratic surveillance has been controversial among some sugarmakers. Naturally independent, they bridle at anyone telling them how to run their operations. It's not that they want to produce anything substandard. In fact, what they serve to their customers also goes into the mouths of their families. It's just that maple syrup has been for so long viewed as inherently safe, and the time-honored processes have not resulted in substantial problems. Of course, any resistance is ironic in a business long in the forefront of protecting products from adulteration and misleading labeling. Although the industry itself has for years been urging more rigorous standards for cleanliness and quality control, the issue sometimes becomes a matter of scale and image.

There's a fear that smaller sugaring operations may disappear under expensive new requirements. Only large producers who can afford shiny new equipment and facilities, and hobbyists, may endure. Lamented by many is further erosion of the syrup-jug backwoods image that is fading in a world of tile floors, washable walls, hairnets, washing stations, and stainless-steel counters. Maple heritage seems to grow in value as technology is more widely adopted.

Food and Drug Administration (FDA) registration requirements issued in 2003 as a response to bioterrorism for facilities that process, pack, or hold food had very little influence on much of the maple world, and few complied or knew if they should. Signed into law in January 2011, the Food Safety Modernization Act enables the FDA to issue regulations for farm manufacturing and packing. More regulations that reach into sugarhouses may be in the offing.

Henry Marckres is not so sure the FDA wants to put a lot of effort into a product that has had so few issues in the past. There are higher priorities. He suspects that voluntary self-regulation by state maple producers associations, combined with modest oversight by state officials, may be workable. Always in the vanguard, the VMSMA recently instituted such a program using a "Sugaring Operations Certification Score Sheet" that covers buildings; food-contact materials such as containers, pumps, and filters; and sanitation, cleaning chemicals, and food allergens.

It may take a little getting used to, but consumers and sugarmakers have a record of looking beyond modernizing changes by emphasizing the product's natural qualities and historic allure. Maple has a message and meaning that sticks. If we are what we eat, an informed public will likely choose maple every time. As one old-timer once remarked, syrup is a distillation of everything that makes trees tall, strong, and solid. Why would anyone want anything else?

Maple Chocolate-Chip Cookies

Yield: about 40 cookies

INGREDIENTS

2 cups white whole-wheat flour
1 teaspoon baking soda
1 teaspoon salt
12 tablespoons unsalted butter
1 cup packed light-brown sugar
⅓ cup hummus

½ cup cane sugar
¼ cup maple syrup
2 large eggs (room temperature)
1 tablespoon vanilla extract
1 cup shredded coconut
1 cup rolled oats

DIRECTIONS

1. Position the oven racks in the top and bottom thirds of the oven. Preheat oven to 350°F.
2. In a medium bowl, whisk flour, baking soda, and salt; set aside.
3. In a separate mixing bowl, beat the butter for 2 minutes at medium speed.
4. To the butter, add the brown sugar and hummus; continue beating another 3 minutes. Beat in the cane sugar and maple syrup for another 2 minutes.
5. Beat in the eggs one at a time, scraping down the sides of the bowl when necessary.
6. Add in the vanilla extract; mix until incorporated.
7. Beat in the coconut, oats, and walnuts until just incorporated.
8. Turn the beaters to low speed and add the flour mixture in three additions.
9. With a rubber spatula, fold in the chocolate chips. Make sure there are no flour patches in the dough.
10. Onto two baking sheets, drop overly full tablespoonfuls of dough, spacing about 2 inches apart. Bake on the top and bottom oven racks for 9 minutes. Reverse trays from top to bottom and back to front. Continue to bake for an additional 9 minutes.
11. Let the cookies cool on the sheets for 2 minutes, then transfer to a wire rack to cool completely. Let cookie sheets cool down for 5–10 minutes before making more cookies.

Recipe by Kathy Palmer

Maple Syrup Oatmeal Cookies

Yield: about 2 dozen cookies

INGREDIENTS

1 cup flour
¼ teaspoon salt
1 teaspoon baking powder
1 cup quick-cooking oats
1 cup walnuts, chopped
½ cup butter
1 large egg
¾ cup maple syrup
½ teaspoon vanilla extract
Shortening (or nonstick spray) for cookie sheet

DIRECTIONS

1. Preheat oven to 375°F. Grease your cookie sheet and set aside.
2. Sift flour, salt, and baking powder together into a bowl. Add the oats and chopped walnuts.
3. In a separate bowl, cream the butter, add the egg, and beat until light. To this, add the maple syrup and vanilla extract. Mix well.
4. Add the flour mixture to the wet ingredients and combine well.
5. Drop by teaspoonfuls onto the greased cookie sheet. Bake at 375° for 8 minutes.

Recipe by Kathy Palmer

Hold Tight and Pray
Character and Place

IT'S A COMMONPLACE that the future of any organization or activity is in its young people. No pursuit can survive unless the next generation takes up the cause or business. But I'm not so sure this is true of sugaring. In the maple world, it may be that the elders of the clan are the future. So many of them are filled with boundless enthusiasm, tireless energy for hard work, and love of craft that they cannot help but inspire anyone of any age who meets them and gets an intoxicating whiff of sweet sugarhouse steam.

Thankfully, sugarmakers are, with some exceptions, long-lived individuals who often keep active well into their eighties and even nineties, so long as they have some help from family, neighbors, and friends. Longevity in maple seems more common than in other occupations or avocations. In fact, older sugarmakers often claim that it's anticipation of the next season that keeps them from the grave. Burr Morse likes to repeat a story told by his friend Robert Howrigan of Fairfield, Vermont, who claimed that "sugarin'" was what kept his grandfather alive. "My grandfather," Howrigan told Burr, "was crippled up with rheumatism and asthma. Several years there he almost died in the winter, but something made him wait. When sugarin' started, they'd draw him up to the sugarhouse on a double sled, and when he got into that steam, he'd be good for another year. I think he'd still be alive had it not been for a late sugar season!"

Sugaring as an activity is filled with anticipation. You have to delight in the mystery of what's next, gamble on change, hoping always that despite difficulties things will get better. Sugarmakers tend to see improved weather ahead, more untapped trees. "You hang tight and pray like hell," octogenarian sugarmaker Al Bolduc of New Portland, Maine, has repeated to me a few times. In the shadow of Sugarloaf Mountain and just outside the ski village of Kingfield with its restaurants and boutiques in old wood-frame buildings, Al has made fifteen hundred to eighteen hundred gallons of syrup a year on over seven thousand taps.

Al is an avuncular, gray-bearded, and cherub-faced man over-flowing with uncommon vivacity and warmth. An easy talker with a quick wit who has a knack for spinning stories, he likes to wear baseball-style caps and has an accent as thick as a down east fog. I hadn't known him more than five minutes before he was telling me a long tale about the moose who stepped out of the woods with yards of blue tubing entangled in his antlers. Shortly thereafter, he offered me "the best advice" he'd ever heard. He took a deep breath and put a hand on my shoulder in a grandfatherly manner. "Before leaving the house always check four things: spectacles, testicles, wallet, and watch," he said, as if it were a kind of Boy Scout motto, motioning to appropriate body parts while ticking off each item.

Al has a gregarious manner and an unusually acute shrewdness about people and the maple business he loves. I first met this back-woods syrup guru at several industry meetings. Until recently, he long represented his state on the North American Maple Syrup Council and the International Maple Syrup Institute, and was a prime mover in both the Maine Maple Producers Association and the Maine Somerset County Sugarmakers Association. I always found Al's en-thusiasm invigorating, but not until I traveled down a dirt road to his story-and-a-half 1809 Greek revival house with a green metal roof did I feel the full force of his passion. In fact, as we walked along a muddy path from his messy desk in an otherwise neat home to the epicenter of his operation at the sugarhouse, his speech became even more animated than usual, his step livelier as he talked about new technology, the changing length of seasons, and the untapped poten-tial of the Somerset County woods.

Growing up on a dairy farm in West Concord, New Hampshire, Al had his first experience with sugaring watching his grandparents. By the time he was in grammar school, he was boiling sap in the back-yard in a flat pan placed over concrete blocks. As a kid during World

War II, when help was scarce, he was put to work with farm chores. He hated milking cows and escaped only when he moved to Connecticut, where his mother had became a Rosie-the-riveter at Pratt & Whitney. He swore he'd "never pull another tit again."

A natural athlete, he played football for Hartford Public High School, but skiing was his passion, and he was good at it. Eventually, he became an international competitor and a first alternate on the 1956 U.S. Olympic ski team. He skied on groomed slopes and rough trails like Mount Washington's Tuckerman Ravine, sometimes with his friend Brooks Dodge, son of the legendary Appalachian Mountain Club woodsman Joe Dodge.

Skiing brought Al to the Sugarloaf area when he was hired to help start a rental, equipment, and clothing business in Kingfield. He bought his fifty-two-acre farm from a bank in the mid-1950s and put out a few buckets. His sugaring was modest for many years because it conflicted with ski season. After three decades, he got out of retail and decided to concentrate on the farm, going from buckets to tubing as his labor force of children grew up and moved away.

You couldn't have a nicer spring day when I visited at the beginning of April a few years ago, but despite his native exuberance Al was a bit confounded by the weather. The season had been preternaturally short. "Anyone on buckets has been done for a few days already, even north of here," he complained. "Well up into Somerset County they're not getting the temperature fluctuations they need. At least there's still snow on the ground in those woods, and where there's snow there's hope." He looked around as we walked, shaking his head. While the summit of Sugarloaf was still as white as a bald eagle's pate, there were only patches of snow in his boggy woods, where usually at this time of year he had three and a half to four feet of the white stuff.

Soon Al seemed to put his tribulations with the weather behind him, and vitality returned to his voice. "It gets into your veins and arteries," he said of sugaring. "It's an almost sacred rite full of spring's excitement. The smell of it gets me energized." He paused in thought a moment. "I remember the family pulling together."

The conversation seemed to seesaw back and fourth between his own operation and the sugaring world generally. "Sugarmakers are

Al Bolduc makes a point

a community," he said instructively. "The more knowledge you gain, the more you want to share." He fed me some details about his RO and his vacuum system, which he kept at twenty-two inches. Technology was causing accelerating obsolescence in a marketplace that was "both subtle and brutal." It was filling new operators with bravado. "They go from greenhorn to expert in just a couple years without enough background to temper their judgment." He stopped walking momentarily and gave me his trademark wink. "Expert," he said disdainfully. "That's an idiot a long way from home."

"Maple schools and operator-friendly equipment" were taking "some of the mystery out of syrup making," he lamented. But "you need RO and vacuum to survive with this crazy changing weather and rising fuel costs. Sad to say, the price of all these gizmos is forcing a lot of smaller commercial guys out." He thought for a minute. As an equipment dealer, he said, he was selling a lot of used buckets, indicating people were still getting in on a hobby scale.

Despite a short season, the real problem was oversupply, he said as we entered the sturdy sugarhouse. It had a metal standing-seam roof and T-111 plywood siding. "The industry is expanding at a prodigious rate, maybe as much as a million taps per year." The sugarhouse interior, with a smooth concrete floor and chipboard walls, was in postseason chaos. Though the stainless evaporator with its big steam hood gleamed, all around was a jumble of barrels, filter press parts, pails, funnels, tools, boxes, plastic jugs, hoses, scoops, curls of tubing, and even some old-fashioned galvanized buckets. Al apologized for the mess and picked up the conversation.

"Growth is fine," he said, "as long as it's deep enough and done for the right reasons. Markets are expanding at a healthy rate, but with more taps coming on line . . ." His voice trailed off, and he paused before resuming. "There're a lot of folks putting capital into new equipment — to the tune of tens of thousands. I guess it's good for dealers, like me." He vacillated between positive and cautionary indicators for the industry, and it seemed to embody the attitude of sugarmakers in general.

"Sugaring is satisfying because of the excitement of the unknown," he said. "You never can predict what kind of season it's going to be — it's a gamble." He plopped down on a box. "Who would have thought red maple tapping would grow so rapidly, but RO makes it possible."

Al paused again with that lost-in-thought look, then bent over and grabbed a plastic spout from an old galvanized bucket filled with them. It was one of Leader's check-valve taps. "Every twenty-five to thirty years there's an idea in the business that's transformative. This spout is one of them. Less bacteria means more sap. Simple as that! Ingenious!" He tossed it back into the bucket as another contrary thought swept through his head. He always seemed to be walking a mental tightrope. "Of course, a throwaway piece of plastic is probably bad for the image of an industry that touts itself as sustainable and environmentally friendly." He shook his head. "Crazy world."

Overtaken with serious health concerns, Al didn't sugar in 2014. But when we talked after the season, he insisted that his strength was returning, and he was determined to be out in the woods and running the evaporator as the days got longer next February. The old buoyancy was back in his voice as he contemplated how many taps he might put out and what kind of help he would need. A Leader equipment dealer, he still believed in check valves. But beyond that, he believed in the power of sugaring to bring order to life and energize him regardless of ailments. Concerned about his health, he nevertheless saw in sugaring a significant part of the cure. It was his passion, and while he might slow down, there were yet roles for him to play.

Having pulled my taps for the final time about a decade ago because of health reasons, I knew exactly what Al meant. It was love of sugaring, its connection to nature and humanity, that drove me to talk with him so many times over the years. It was the reason I was telling his tale, and that of so many other sugarmakers.

Al epitomizes the fatalistic optimism of sugarmakers. Their world is an unsteady balance of upbeat expectancy tempered by an onslaught of change and downside indicators like syrup oversupply, fickle weather, technological cost, and threats like the Asian longhorned beetle. And the rate of change is accelerating, leading to further stress. As Russ Davenport observed, "In my lifetime maple sugaring has seen more progress than in the hundreds of years during the early involvement in this process."

Sugarmakers are a study in contrast and juxtaposition. They maintain one of the most ancient, simple, and natural agricultural traditions, yet survival as a commercial operation requires use of increasingly sophisticated technical innovations. Strong and resilient like the trees they tap, they may find more importance in the work itself than in the resulting syrup. For many, the golden liquid or money is almost a byproduct of what they really value. "Maple builds character," Al said, "and there are a lot of characters in maple."

In a sugarmaker's world there is forever next year, always some tinkering that will improve efficiency, more trees to tap. If climate change is heralding a warmer world and the end of sugaring, at least in more southerly regions, sugarmakers may be among the last to give in, regardless of what the timing and length of season indicates. They'll fight with every bit of hard work, technology, and old-timey pluck they can muster.

The challenge facing sugaring may be a good indicator of what is happening to our planet, but more significantly, the persistence of sugarmakers in the face of changes is a measure of the human spirit, the character of a region and a culture, and what it takes to survive. With their sensitivity to subtle changes in the natural world, sugarmakers have an acute sense of the present even as they have one foot in the past and another in the future. In sugaring, there is an unusually tight connection between what is, what was, and what will be. Perhaps that's what we need most as a society if we are to survive the onslaught of change and adaptation ahead.

Sometimes the season ends in disappointment and spoiled sap. But sugarmakers remain undaunted, are constitutionally determined that out of even the worst season something beneficial will arise. It's partially that undying hope that next year's weather will be better—but more than that, there's faith that a bad season will fertilize innovation, induce harder work, or sew the seeds of a marketing breakthrough. Perhaps that outlook was best expressed by John Burroughs, a turn-of-the-twentieth-century Catskill naturalist who one September came upon a sap bucket left beside a maple tree. "It was unspeakably loathsome; there were remains of birds and mice in it; it reeked of corruption. How could innocent rain-water, or maple sap become so foul? It had been cut off from the vital processes; it had been idle; it had taken no part in the work of the seasons." He kicked it over and held his nose. "It seemed as if the very ground would cry out in protest. But a few days of the active chemistry of nature, and all will be pure again." Such is the conviction, the aspiration, and trust of sugarmakers everywhere.

It's by our taking part in the "work of the seasons" and "vital processes" that human temperament and landscape become fused, creating a true essence of place, a unity of humanity and topography. Regardless of what any sugaring year brings, it always reveals the character of this region called New England.

Maple Indian Pudding

Yield: 6–8 servings

INGREDIENTS

Canola oil (or nonstick cooking spray)
3 cups milk
⅔ cup maple syrup
½ cup cornmeal
4 teaspoons butter or margarine
½ teaspoon ground cinnamon
¼ teaspoon ground ginger
¼ teaspoon ground nutmeg
Pinch of salt
3 large eggs, beaten
Whipped cream or maple syrup, for serving

DIRECTIONS

1. Preheat oven to 350°F.
2. Lightly coat a 1-quart ovenproof casserole dish with canola oil or cooking spray.
3. In a large saucepan, bring milk to a boil over medium heat. Reduce heat to low, stir in the maple syrup, and cook for 4 minutes.
4. Add cornmeal and cook, stirring constantly, for 6–8 minutes. Add butter, cinnamon, ginger, nutmeg, and salt, stirring constantly.
5. Remove from heat and let cool 5 minutes.
6. Whisk eggs in a bowl, then whisk into the milk mixture until well combined.
7. Pour mixture into oiled casserole dish and place on middle rack of the oven.
8. Bake 1 hour or until the center is set.
9. Serve warm. Top with whipped cream and/or drizzle with a little additional maple syrup, if desired.

Recipe by Kay Carroll

Maple Bourbon Sour

Yield: 2 servings

INGREDIENTS

6 tablespoons bourbon

2 tablespoons maple syrup

2 tablespoons fresh lemon juice

DIRECTIONS

1. Combine the ingredients, stirring to mix well.
2. Pour the mixture into a cocktail shaker filled with ice and shake well.
3. Strain the mixture into two glasses.

Acknowledgments

. . . .

I AM A FORTUNATE MAN to have been a sugarmaker and to spend so much time among sugarmakers. It's doubtful that one could find another group of people so uncommonly welcoming, naturally curious, hardworking, aware of their heritage, and engaged with both nature and technology. As a writer, it was impossible to know people of such energy, probity, and worth without writing a book about them. They have been my inspiration for this project, and for many other unrelated endeavors.

I am deeply indebted to Dr. Michael Farrell, director of Cornell's Uihlein Forest, for reading through my manuscript and offering suggestions both literary and technical. He is not only an expert on things maple, but a fine writer. I also extend my gratitude to my wife, Mary C. Fletcher, for sharing her keen insights about some of the sugarmakers we visited together, and for reading the final draft and making it flow more smoothly. This is a much better book because of their input. Nevertheless, there are bound to be mistakes, for which I take full responsibility.

I am truly grateful to all those in the sugaring world who so generously shared with me their expertise, opinions, and wisdom. I have spent many hours with some and had brief conversations with others. All were valuable. My one regret is that I could not include between the covers of this book all the great stories I've been told. I'd like to completely detail the specifics of my encounters with all the maple people I've met and the kindnesses done me in the course of my five-year adventure researching sugaring, but that would take hundreds of pages. Unfortunately, I'm limited to mentioning just the names of some of those who have given me the gift of their stories and advice. If I have forgotten anyone, please accept my deepest apologies.

Heartfelt thanks go to the following: Jason Anderson, Erica Andrews, Brian Atwood, George L. Bailey Jr., Paul K. Barten, Bruce Bascom, Bud Bemis, Mike Bennett, Benjamin Berecz, Mark B. Bigelow, Alfred Bolduc, Ernie and Armand Bolduc, Ray Bonenberg, Kevin and Kristi Brannen, Steve Broderick, Jody Bronson, Richard Brown, Thomas E. Buck, Charles Canham, Arlow Case, Dave Chapeskie, Charlie Chase, Stephen L. Childs, Bob Chutter, Jim Civitello, Alvin and David Clark, Wilson "Bill" Clark, Rand Cooper, Joyce Corso, Renaud Y. Couture, Ted Cowles, Russ Davenport, James Dina, Dana Dix, Chuck Drake, Jerry Dubie, Pat and Bob Dubos, Bill Eva, Richard Faucher, Ben Fisk, Gary Graham, Bradley C. Gillilan, Bruce Gillilan, Michael A. Girard and Michael L. Girard, Henry Grape, Gary J. Gaudette, Scott and Colleen Goeben, Jim Graves, J. Mark Harran, Scott Heth, Bob Howe, Paul M. Hughes, Brian Hutchinson, Bernard Jolin, Debbie and Russ Jordan, Jay Kaplan, Ray Kasulaitis, Peter Lamb, Jinny Lamontagne and Odette Gilbert, Rob and Jean Lamothe, Barbara M. Lassonde, Vincent Lavorgna, Ray Leonard Jr., Betty Ann and Don Lockhart, Mark Mankin, Henry J. Marckres, Rick Marsh, Vic Mastro, Clint D. McFarland, Lyle Merrifield, Gerard Milne, Burr and Tom Morse, Rich Munch, Larry Myott, Avis and Rich Norman, Jean-Claude Pare, Wayne Palmer, Timothy D. Perkins, Hank Peterson, Fred Petig, Geoffrey Picard, Winton Pitcoff, Robert Poirier, Bernard Rodrigue, Guy Rodrigue, Chris Russo, Mart Sprague, Jeremy Steeves, Mike Stevens, Christian Stromberg, Barb Sweet, Jack Trumbull, Abby van den Berg, Kirsten M. Walker, Timothy R. Wilmot, Joyce and Ron Wenzel.

My special appreciation goes to Kay Carroll, a member of the Connecticut Maple Syrup Producers Association board of directors, for permission to use recipes from *The Maple Cookbook: Connecticut Style*, including some of her own. Thanks also to the following, whose recipes were used: Karen Broderick, Betsey Dalton, Pat Dubos, Susan Derby, Carolyn Gimbrone, Midge Harvey, Shirley Hewlett, Rob and Jean Lamothe, Nancy Reynolds, Trevor Soulé, Kirsten Walker, and the Wenzel Sugarhouse. Thanks also to April Jones for her excellent editorial assistance preparing the recipes for this book, and to Glenn Novak for his brilliant copyediting.

Garnet Books

Titles with asterisks (*) are also in the Driftless Connecticut Series

Garnet Poems:
An Anthology of Connecticut
Poetry Since 1776*
Dennis Barone, editor

Food for the Dead:
On the Trail of New England's Vampires
Michael E. Bell

The Case of the Piglet's Paternity:
Trials from the New Haven Colony,
1639–1663*
Jon C. Blue

Early Connecticut Silver, 1700–1840
Peter Bohan and
Philip Hammerslough

The Connecticut River:
A Photographic Journey through
the Heart of New England
Al Braden

Tempest-Tossed:
The Spirit of Isabella Beecher Hooker
Susan Campbell

Connecticut's Fife & Drum Tradition*
James Clark

Sunken Garden Poetry, 1992–2011
Brad Davis, editor

Rare Light:
J. Alden Weir in Windham, Connecticut,
1882–1919
Anne E. Dawson, editor

The Old Leather Man:
Historical Accounts of a Connecticut
and New York Legend
Dan W. DeLuca, editor

Post Roads & Iron Horses:
Transportation in Connecticut from
Colonial Times to the Age of Steam*
Richard DeLuca

The Log Books:
Connecticut's Slave Trade
and Human Memory*
Anne Farrow

Dr. Mel's Connecticut Climate Book
Dr. Mel Goldstein

Hidden in Plain Sight:
A Deep Traveler Explores Connecticut
David K. Leff

Maple Sugaring:
Keeping It Real in New England
David K. Leff

Becoming Tom Thumb:
Charles Stratton, P. T. Barnum, and
the Dawn of American Celebrity*
Eric D. Lehman

Homegrown Terror:
Benedict Arnold and the Burning
of New London*
Eric D. Lehman

Westover School:
Giving Girls a Place of Their Own
Laurie Lisle

Heroes for All Time:
Connecticut's Civil War Soldiers
Tell Their Stories*
Dione Longley and Buck Zaidel

ABOUT THE AUTHOR

David K. Leff is a former deputy commissioner
at the Connecticut Department of Environmental
Protection. He is a poet and essayist and the author
of several books, including *Hidden in Plain Sight: A Deep
Traveler Explores Connecticut.* His work has appeared in
the *Hartford Courant, Appalachia, Yankee, Canoe & Kayak,*
the *Encyclopedia of New England,* and elsewhere. Leff
was a maple sugarmaker for a over a dozen years
and served on the board of the Maple Syrup
Producers Association of Connecticut.

. . . . .